If You Came This Way

Also by Peter Davis

Hometown
Where is Nicaragua?

If You Came This Way

A JOURNEY THROUGH
THE LIVES OF THE UNDERCLASS

PETER DAVIS

JOHN WILEY & SONS, INC.
New York · Chichester · Brisbane · Toronto · Singapore

Copyright © 1995 by Peter Davis
Published by John Wiley & Sons, Inc.

Library of Congress Cataloging-in-Publication Data:

Davis, Peter, 1937–
    If you came this way : a journey through the lives of the underclass / Peter Davis.
        p. cm.
    Includes index.
    ISBN 0-471-11074-4 (alk. paper)
    1. Poor—United States—Case studies. I. Title.
HC110.P6D383   1995
305.5′69′0973—dc20   95-12872

Printed in the United States of America

10 9 8 7 6 5 4 3 2

For Karen

We are not concerned with the very poor. They are unthinkable, and only to be approached by the statistician or the poet.

E. M. FORSTER, *Howards End*

The territorial aristocracy of former ages was either bound by law, or thought itself bound by usage, to come to the relief of its serving-men and to relieve their distresses. But the manufacturing aristocracy of our age first impoverishes and debases the men who serve it and then abandons them to be supported by the charity of the public.

ALEXIS DE TOCQUEVILLE, *Democracy in America*

Poverty is the parent of revolution and crime.

ARISTOTLE, *Politics*

Contents

Preface

No matter how well I think I've laid out my route, I am forever running into a combination of the unexpected and the exotic. The second time I saw Kelso Dana Jr., he had just tried to rob a drugstore, not with any weapon, basically just filching. Gently and sheepishly, he was handing back a few shoplifted notions to the assistant manager. I found myself embarrassed for this kid, identifying with him mistakenly. I say mistakenly because of course I knew nothing, absolutely nothing as yet, about Kelso Dana Jr. except that with his wide-eyed gaze at the assistant manager, and his attempt to arrange his mouth into a brave, crooked little smile, he hooked me.

We always learn when we travel, and what we learn seems to be mostly about ourselves. My encounters with the underclass are personal: They are about me and my developing interests as much as they are about the people I met. If I need one, my excuse is context: What is a journey without an emotional itinerary? What are travels without a traveler? I have always been compelled to search outside myself to find precisely what I'm feeling inside. In my compulsion to learn about others—terminal voyeurism?—I never cease to be surprised by their terrors, jokes, strategies, and motives.

No less than anyone else, I am a prisoner of class, circumstance, and one sort of partiality or another, all of which shape my responses regardless of how hard I try to transcend them. Conditioning imposes qualms I had to shed like any other excess baggage. Wondering about the underclass, I wondered about their restraints, so incomparably more confining than mine. I'd grown dissatisfied with the theoretical and doctrinal wrangling over the poor, full of feverish rhetoric and zealotry, and I had to see for myself. There must, I thought, be more to the underclass than the sum of pedagogical abstraction.

The people I came to know in all their particularity have existed on the American canvas throughout our history. Our greatest writers have portrayed them. Huckleberry Finn was an underclass runaway; so was Jim. The people we think of as underclass have been part of American society, defining features in their way, through a variety of incarnations. I've protected the identities of my companions on this journey, but I tried to be faithful to the names they conveyed to me. Dinah Lou Freeman, Sherry Lane, Adriana St. Duclos Mathere, Ronnielee Divine, Kelso Dana Jr.: They become recognizable not because of any gifts of mine but because they are there, here, part of us, and always have been.

In at least one case I stumbled upon a person who seemed to have been invented by the author who perhaps best exemplifies the continuum of Americana. Hector Zacario, though a Mexican-American from Texas instead of a white drifter from Missouri, has so many of the unlovable traits, even the prejudices, of Huckleberry Finn's father that I had to ask him at one point in our estranged relationship if he had ever heard of Mark Twain. "Sure I know the sonofabitch," he barked without hesitation. "He's that Anglo spy for the welfare downtown."

We fasten no seat belts here; on this journey we find our way with a range of feeling—empathy, rage, admiration, fear, frustration, resolve. There is no 12-step program for poverty. There are only the poor themselves, one by one by one.

If You Came This Way

1

Is This Trip Necessary?

Introduction and quiz: Who is the underclass? They're not you and they're not me. They are our enemies, and they know it even if we don't. I would have denied this before. I wasn't aware of an inherent hostility between classes, or perhaps I was and I wasn't. I did not, certainly, admit it until I took a journey through their world, a journey to an American hell.

I went there after being mugged. A blurred ghost out of the shadows, a nylon stocking over its head. Metal glinting in my eyes. My wife fumbling in her purse. Would he hurt us? The metal again, dull, dim, up under my nose. A .45, thick, potent, military. Our wallets in his hand. He's gone.

This was at night on a sidewalk in New York City, a few feet from our own apartment, described by the police as a garden-variety heist, just your basic mugger with a stocking over his head. The mugging did not launch me on the trip to the underclass, not by itself. A carnal aspect to the incident—inescapable, frightening, tempting—would not let me alone. I was provoked, curious, curiously lured. The mugging started a process that brought me to the decision.

Is it not possible to get excited about a problem until it comes home? Of course, there are those whose combination of personal fervor, emotion, religion, ambition, and ideology drives them to commitment. There is no record that Gandhi, Mother Teresa, or Martin Luther King was ever on the brink of starvation, yet they all became tribunes of the dispossessed. Most of us are not crusaders. I'm not. Most of us find it difficult to care, for very long, about what doesn't directly affect us. I do. I've seldom dwelt more than passingly on these other people, these people in the underclass, especially when their otherness seems so total. I can be sympathetic and cerebral but not passionate and pained until I'm threatened close up, face to face with the enemy.

As the days passed after the mugging, I began to think about what would have to happen in my own life to bring me to the point where I would confront two adults on the sidewalk with a gun in my hand and demand their money. Hardly immune to social sloth, periods in which I dream that everyone and everything in America are sort of improving on their own, I suddenly felt violated in my civic certainties. Conditions I had grown to accept became a menace. What had been sad became urgent. Possibly I only wanted to see the face of the man who had scared me so much. Maybe he was more afraid of me than I was of him. I decided to find him. To find—more accurately, more feasibly—the kind of person who had mugged me, his background, his family, his home if he had one. If my mugger had been in a police lineup with, say, an undersecretary of state, an NFL lineman, and a neighborhood patrolman—each of whom I may have glimpsed once or twice—I could never have identified which one had mugged me. Yet he had identified me so easily. My trip to find him, this generic desperado from the underclass, was conceived as a way to restore my own sense of who I am in the society that surrounds me. The trick would be doing this so I would enter another America feet first, with the rest of me following, as an inquisitive traveler, not a disguised Yupster gone slumming.

Much later, finished with my research—alleys, soup lines, empty faces, broken faces, faces of the American damned—I went for a walk in the woods on a crisp September morning when the leaves had begun to turn. I live in Maine now, where the fall comes early, and the butterfly I saw must have known it would either not last long in

Maine or not last long at all. As the butterfly made ready to leave—the state or the earth, I couldn't tell—it seemed to enjoy itself perfectly, heedlessly. Rainbow wings, sailing into the wind, movements like darts of a laser beam. The air was lost in pigment. I followed the butterfly as it dipped away from me, swooped under a branch, dived back in my direction. It was happy, beautiful, free—and I wanted to smash it.

The point was: How dare any part of creation belong so cheerfully to itself when the misery I'd been observing—even, at times, convincing myself I was sharing—was so complete? How easily, in the end, I'd escaped it! Such an escape, the escape back to places where grace and beauty are daily possibilities, remained light years beyond the reach of the people whose lives I'd been trying to understand, people for whom "freedom" is not merely an abstraction but a term of mockery. I was ashamed when I realized I had never even contemplated them as fellow citizens. Fellows are peers who can do for each other. When I thought about it, these Americans and I offer each other virtually nothing.

For these fellow citizens I'd been with, learning to read, finding a home, stopping drugs, being accepted into job training can be achievements as significant as that of a paralyzed accident victim who slowly, agonizingly, learns to wiggle a single toe. The obstacles to basic survival can be colossal, Himalayan. For many of those I had lived among, getting onto welfare or even committing a crime—my mugging, for instance—would be a leap upward from where they are. A criminal act, however antisocial from the perspective of the state, would be *an act,* an assertion of self, a pledge toward betterment that is, for many of those I met, well beyond their reach. They have far more crimes committed against them than they can even conceive of committing. Freedom, rarely a collective proposition, is mine in abundance, but they experience it—at a distant remove, vicariously—mostly when they watch television commercials or get high. Which means, by any definition I can relate to, they are not free at all.

This book takes you on my journey into the underclass. Also

known as the persistently poor, the chronically poor, and, lately, the outerclass. Whatever we call them (when we bother to call them anything), they constitute a class whose very existence is appalling because it is not *supposed* to exist in America. Yet the United Nations Development Programme reports that even Bangladesh has managed to immunize a greater percentage of its children against diphtheria than we have. The U.N. report was itself a kind of affliction for me, as it had been for the columnist Murray Kempton when he looked at the same figures: "A nation that we think of as hopeless struggles to make life a little better; and the nation that is the repository of our hopes indifferently watches it get worse for millions of our helpless own."

Meet our helpless own. Watch as what passes for their lives belies the myth of equal opportunity in America. My journey into the underclass, like all travels, was more about understanding than about seeing the sights. Yet it is the sights and smells, the images of perennial poorness, that I can't shake. The widow found with her legs frozen in her own urine after the heat was shut off, the family of six fighting with rats over rotten potatoes, the brother and sister arrested after killing a traveling businessman for his pocket change. I tell you about these people not to be sadistic, not to make you guilty in your complacency, not to present the smug machismo of the war correspondent filing a report from hell. I note these blighted lives out of the conviction—no, the fear—that where the underclass is concerned, what we don't know can destroy us as their reality is destroying them.

My journey left me with one dead certainty. This certainty was hard for me to learn and acknowledge, but it is what anyone in the underclass knows instinctively as a child. Wealth is not all that is inherited in America. So is poverty.

A person could always be born poor in America, as in any country, but we have now produced and devised means to maintain a poverty caste, an inherent underclass who are locked into their station and out of any other by virtually every institution they come in contact with. Even after my journey among them, it is not easy for me to count how many times a day, in how many ways, in how many efforts to do anything legal, these Americans are locked out. Forget, for a moment, about knowing how to read, or possessing basic skills, or even having an address. What about finding a place to bathe or shave, an article of clothing that fits and isn't torn, a meal that doesn't leave you hungry, so that when you try to get work you don't stink with something beyond sweat that we in the employing classes may recognize as hopelessness? What about having faith in nothing but your own inadequacy? These are the persistently poor. Their horizon has shriveled to a smashed window, a hungry baby's wail, a pebble of crack.

I hadn't gone far in my preparations, trying to make sense of the tangle between deprivation and public policy, when I realized that at no time in this century have the poor been our enemies to the extent they are now. It is not merely that we turn our backs to the very poor while we debate the most sanitary way of disposing of them and simultaneously spending less money on welfare. The enmity is personal. It's "us" against "them". We dread "them" as we walk to our cars, step over a body in the subway, hurry away from the cash machine. We build, one by one, on each other's enmity until it has become national. Only the elderly can remember when the poor were even poorer, when they were more numerous, when the Great Depression leveled the working class. But then the poor were so many of "us." Now the poor, specifically the persistently neglected poor whom I came to know best, are declaratively, definitively "them." I shun them, I fear them, and, as with any enemy, I cancel them out of my thinking whenever possible.

The consequence of so many with so little is a new cold war spreading over the land. Like the old cold war, there is always the menace that it can become hot, violent, deadly. And there are the brush fires we see on television and read about daily, little conflagrations that remind us of what lurks in the shadows. We in the many middle classes feel ourselves victimized by addicts, paupers, beggars, muggers. For us, the poor have replaced the Communists as our principal enemies. Even during the old cold war, much of the hysteria against Reds and presumed Reds was connected to a fear of the poor overthrowing the rich. With few communist states on the global horizon, with almost no Left on the domestic front, the poor have become our targets. The war on poverty of the '60s has become the war against the poor of the '90s.

And how do the poor see you and me, especially the most wretched of the poor who have never known either plenty or its prospect? I have found that these most damaged and undefended of our countrymen look at the rest of the United States, particularly the *official* United States, as an armed force attacking them. For them the cold war is already hot. "Every day I wake up, don't matter if it's in a shelter or under some bridge," a woman in Santa Monica told me, her chin cut and her straw hair matted but her eyes clear and doleful, "and it's like this cavalry's charging down on me, going to hoof me under good." Santa Monica, where I was born, was a town I'd always thought of as one of California's gentlest, its people mirrored in its ocean: pacific. Yet there and everywhere, members of the underclass have used terms from combat to describe the rest of America to me. The marines are coming to get them; they will be strafed; heavy artillery is being brought up against them; the infantry is advancing; the mayor called in an air strike on them when he closed the downtown shelter.

I came to the underclass with questions. Who are they? Quite beyond my own—after all, harmless—mugging, why do I perceive this class that is scarcely more than litter on our landscape as a threat? What made them? Why should we care? If we do bother about them at all, what can be done?

Other guidebooks tell you how to capture the essence of your visit in an image. See the Iglesia di Santa Vittoria just after first light, if you can get the sexton to open the portals for you when the sun streams through the stained glass windows to give the human figures their most glorious incarnation. Here, with the underclass, you can use any moment for its reflection on the damnation of those you visit. See the lunch line outside the Salvation Army in Bangor, Maine, start to form shortly after 10:00 A.M. on a February morning, all dripping noses and shuffling feet and holes at the elbows, when the winter seems interminable, the berry-packing jobs that temporarily sustain the vagrant or migrant infinitely far in both the past and the future. The difficulty of doing anything about inherited poverty is introduced by our difficulty in understanding it, in accepting it into our psyches. "Inherited poverty" seems a contradiction in American terms, a violation of our destiny. If you come from a middle-class background, a background even of struggle and occasional unemployment, you come from a background underpinned and legislated by hope. That makes a crime of despair, which becomes almost as hard for us to understand, or discuss intelligently, as sex was for the Victorians.

Much of the underclass is still invisible, holed up in shelters, manacled to ghettos, hidden in rural hollows. But many of the underclass, or persistently poor, unlike the terrified millions staring into the abyss of poverty but still above it, are in your face. The man who lives on the subway steps, the two women who huddle together in the doorway of the dry cleaner's, the family that sleeps in the park just outside your children's playground. How often can you ride a subway, walk on a crowded street, leave a theater late at night, use a bathroom in a public park, or even walk in that same park after sundown, without being approached by someone who asks for and sometimes demands the money you worked for and he did not? You feel assaulted, first by the panhandler, next by guilt, finally by rage.

Confidently assuming the rightability of wrongs, I have been a liberal or beyond all my life. But as far as the underclass is concerned, the *unreached* underclass, what good has that done? How can it be that in this country, the country I have an abiding though open-eyed faith in, a whole class of people can be consigned to a socioeconomic graveyard? Is it their fault? Is it our fault?

For now, I will make the simple assertion that we have not only abandoned but also condemned the least able, the least educated, the least successful among us. Can the society call itself great that does not assure to its disadvantaged food, clothing, shelter, medical care, and a chance to work? The poor are a judgment and a prophecy; they accurately if embarrassingly describe our concerns, define our goals, highlight the signature on our social contract.

The underclass—"Under" what? Under the rest of us, of course—challenges everyone, dares us, to care. By the nervous standards of middle-class morality, a promiscuous phrase granting its favors as readily to satire as self-congratulation, the underclass undermines. Its members are said to wander around aimlessly, they watch acres of TV, they drop babies here and there like bottle caps, they do an astonishing amount of drugs, and their thirst is reputedly unquenchable.

When I became interested in exploring the depths of this underworld, I realized how far away I was from understanding real poverty. For this subject, this inquiry, this search, I have a background that looks, at first, both unsuitable and unsympathetic. Growing up, I was a child of some privilege. At one house we had a pool, at another a tennis court. Yet it was shaky privilege.

My father was a screenwriter, a calling that has notable downs to accompany its occasional ups. In the totem pole of who was invited where when I was growing up, screenwriting was above stuntman, below associate producer. A screenwriter's job possibilities were uncertain, and screenwriters themselves never mattered much in the Hollywood hierarchy of my childhood, the '40s and '50s. They liked to say of their work, citing the Bible, that in the beginning was the word. This was not strictly true, however, even though a script clearly preceded the shooting of a film. For the motion picture industry, in the beginning was the meeting. Was and is. Screenwriters were seldom even present then at the initial meeting, and if they were, they certainly never ran it. Then, too, an important part of the job description was toadying. "What a fabulous idea, Harry, it'll be delicious right after the seduction at the start of the third act." I know my father didn't like that part of his work, and he did like to say he wasn't good at it, but people were fond of him and sought his scripts, and as I mentioned, he did well enough for me to have been a child of some privilege.

Still, my own history of defining "poor" made me think I knew something about the poor, about how they are like everyone else, about how they are different. In my background were the Okies, the Axis, the pickers, and HUAC. They all taught me something and left me ignorant.

As a boy on a California ranch, I went to school with children known to everyone, including themselves, as Okies and Arkies, their families having come west out of the Dustbowl. They wore no shoes to school even in winter, even when it was cold enough for their fathers to be lighting smudgepots in the orange groves every night. Though I knew our family had more and they had less, I played with them as equals and don't recall feeling sorry for them until my parents began to give them my old clothing. Tow-headed riffraff, my grandfather called my playmates. Noses always running.

Their families had come to California to pick not only oranges but grapes, lemons, and cherries. The cherries were grown by the few Japanese families who prospered in San Bernardino County before World War II, which, when it came, removed them from their cherry orchards. I knew the four Japanese children at our school, first as friends, then as enemies. Then they disappeared. We were taught this was unjust, but we were glad they were gone. Their fields lay uncultivated, they were gone, and we heard they were in camps behind barbed wire. They must be the new poor.

The Okies and Arkies were the old poor, and they were the poor poor. These children were a little wild, ungovernable, but also, I reflect now, somewhat resigned even at 9 and 10. It was the wildness, of course, that I liked. The doctor's son, the police chief's son, and I talked about what we might be when we grew up. The sons of pickers, I now recall though I ignored it then, talked only about the weekend and the fort we'd build and the enemy planes we'd pretend to shoot down, not about the adult future. The daughters of pickers, no bones about it, were studying washing and ironing. Yet if you had asked me I'd have said that my classmates' opportunities were equal—almost—to mine. Silly boy. What a gulf there was between me and these children I played with every day in school. I saw something real in them but also couldn't see it. I suppose it would have been too painful for me to understand how many ways they were not getting the chances I was. Perhaps we have to project an equality of opportunity onto the poor in order not to be horrified at precisely how deprived of opportunity they are.

While we lived on the ranch the only Latino or Hispanic—but we called them Mexicans then, as they called themselves—I knew was from Alta Loma and managed a lemon grove for my father, who was a gentleman rancher sort of and a well-paid screenwriter really. The Mexican's name was, of course, Jesus. He was not poor. He looked down on the Okies and refused to hire them, preferring his compatriots, who were so poor they often wore rags. We saw the Mexicans as poor—and scary—because they were foreigners. I thought many of them looked diseased, and whatever they had I didn't want to be near it. The native born fearing and misunderstanding the immigrants: I repeated that ancient pattern with the Mexicans.

Later, our lemons were picked by German prisoners of war, who also looked poor because they were the enemy brought low, and we exulted. I decided that the enemies of the United States, first the Japanese and now the Germans, the major Axis powers, would become poor *because they were enemies.* (Today the underclass are our enemies *because they are poor.*) I have never seen anything so shiny as the gold front tooth of Jesus as he smiled while wreaking vengeance on the Germans by ordering them to pick faster. "*Andale! Andale!*"

But "poor" was always relative because I didn't—couldn't, really—know what poverty consists of for those who endure it daily. I did know, though, that "poor" was to be feared and avoided. By the time I was a teenager we had moved back to where the motion picture business actually was, and "poor" meant kids whose fathers were chased by HUAC, the House Un-American Activities Committee. HUAC slid into place as the villain of my teenage years, replacing the vanquished Axis who had been the villain of my boyhood. A variety of organizations calling themselves patriotic, led by HUAC, promoted a movie business blacklist for anyone suspected of communist sympathies. (I didn't know then that people in many other occupations were also targeted.) That was Beverly Hills in the '50s. We felt sorry for them, the children of the blacklistees, and superior to them. They seemed to become poor in a hurry, some of them disappearing to Mexico almost as fast as the Japanese had disappeared to camps a decade earlier. "Poor," as I said, was relative, but someone who lost a swimming pool seemed as deserving of sympathy in my adolescence as someone with no shoes had in my childhood.

The blacklist was an occupational hazard of the movie business— "like venereal disease for the other kind of whore," a self-despising screenwriter told my father—and it had nothing to do with how good an American or screenwriter you thought you were. When my own father eventually got blacklisted, my family shifted gears. Our attitude remained the same toward those we regarded as poor, only now we aimed the attitude in the direction of home. We felt sorry for ourselves, *and* we also felt superior to ourselves. During that time we were alienated from the rich, the families whose breadwinners still drew $5,000 a week—both more and less—as well as from the truly needy, which we were not and whom we never dared identify with anyway.

But of course we weren't really poor, we just felt that way compared with how we had felt before. Frozen peas and a Pontiac instead of fresh artichokes and a Chrysler. The buckles on our tightened belts were no longer silver but still brass. When I went to college, my parents were able to manage the tuition at Harvard. Poor people underwent still another transition for me, becoming the Irish. I noblessly tutored two of them, little Bobby and even littler Caroline, in the projects, as their matchbox brick housing was called. Even while I was doing a reasonably nice thing, my alienation from the poor was perfecting itself: I was trying to help them; therefore, they couldn't be like me because look how much they needed my help.

One Saturday I invited Bobby to visit my roommates and me, probably less an exercise in generosity than vanity. He didn't know what to say, we didn't know what to do with him, and nervousness soon gave way on both sides to boredom. The other poor people I knew in Cambridge, or rather never took the trouble to know, were called "biddies." They cleaned our rooms and, yes, made our beds. Five dollars at Christmas: that was as much attention as my biddy, Mrs. Ahearn, ever received from me. She could have been Bobby's or Caroline's grandmother; her dyed red hair had grown out so much the gray washed up under the red like a tide that wouldn't be stopped.

After I grew up, for 30 years in New York the very poor meant the people I was scared of, the people who threaten people like me. They were threatening not because they wanted our jobs or competed in any way that was meaningful to either us or them, but only because they threatened us physically.

When we walked down the street they at least cadged and at most mugged us. As the '80s wore on, you couldn't walk the few blocks from the subway stop to our apartment without fielding at least six requests for change. When they were young, my older sons were routinely relieved of their bus passes at knifepoint, sometimes on West 86th Street, or Amsterdam Avenue, once on Park Avenue at 79th Street, where my then-16-year-old was beaten up because he did *not* have a bus pass. It had already been stolen by somebody else. Before we moved uptown we lived in Greenwich Village, where our apartment was burglarized three times in six years. My younger children, born in the '80s, learned how to step deftly over the homeless, politely pretending not to notice, on their way to school or a play date. When my wife and I were finally mugged, we were underneath our own apartment awning. I couldn't see anything but the .45 as I made the jittery grope for my wallet.

I never blamed New York. We had already decided to move to Maine before the sidewalk robbery. I loved New York the whole time I lived there. The mugging was because of the poor, not the city. It's satisfying to think I tend to support progressive social programs because I am generous and want to help those who have less than I. But who am I to think I'm so generous? I'm not in fact so generous.

As I try to understand my feelings and motives toward the poor, I'm forced to see that part of me hates them. I owe a good deal of my support for "progressive" poverty solutions to that hatred. I hate them so much I want to do away with them. Besides, we all suspect that what they have is catching.

2

Packing for
the Journey

The view of poverty as contagious, as having the stench of terminal illness, leads us to take sanctuary in the word "underclass," which must mean someone else because it certainly doesn't refer to me. A voyage of discovery is always a voyage to the self; Columbus was unlikely to have known about his hostility to non-Europeans until he met some. Then they could be safely dealt with as "savages." Once I'm satisfied that those in this "underclass" are safely other than I am, I can afford to think about where they came from.

Looking for answers, looking for questions, I took a kind of radar scan of the available wisdom. Among professionals, theories about extreme poverty detonate into intellectual Roman candles. Everyone has a surmise, a premise, an explanation, a conclusion. The welfare system grows vegetables; as the poor become dependent on it, they lose all initiative. The rich got richer in the '80s, running away from the poor, sucking the nourishment from inner cities until only shells remained. Progress hates the poor; it has rendered them obsolete. Our industrial base has vanished and along with it the market for menial labor, leaving the poorest poor not only unemployed but unemployable. Another contention is that the poor were once enabled by education, but are now abandoned by the schools even before they drop out. Voices rain opinions on us about the poor as if we were standing under the Tower of Babel. The problem is economic; no, it's geographic; no, it's technological; not a chance, it's all about race. Everywhere a diagnosis, nowhere a cure. If you don't blame poverty on the poor themselves (always an enticing option), you are left with a variety of choices, all revolving around "the system." It is the system of welfare if you're conservative, of racism if you're a liberal, of capitalism if you're a radical, of a postindustrial society that no longer needs unskilled workers if you're an economist, of institutional unemployment and a vanished work ethic if you're a ghetto theorist, of population movements into and out of big cities if you're a social ornithologist tracking migratory trends. Each approach has some plausibility, doesn't it? The litany of theories explains the underclass away without touching the people trapped in it.

In the teeth of confusing claims and theories, and a policy gridlock that has paralyzed action on behalf of the persistently poor for over a decade, I wanted to find out who and what we're arguing over. Is race incidental, coincidental, accidental, or at the heart of the heart of the problem? My journey to the underclass could let me see whom we're coddling or neglecting, where the problem is, why it became this serious, and possibly how we might begin to find remedies.

I looked at poverty once before, in the late '60s—an auspicious moment for those who thought they could do something about America's unkept promises. The problems of the republic did not seem so intractable then, did they? The particular issue was hunger, and I roamed the country to research a documentary film about white, black, brown, and red children with shrunken limbs and swollen bellies, families who never saw fresh meat or vegetables, communities with inadequate food programs. Some parents were too proud to admit there was a problem because, just as it is now un-American to declare people born into a poverty caste, it was then un-American to admit that in the affluent society you didn't have enough to eat, and worse, couldn't feed your young. Hunger in America was widespread in the '60s, afflicting 10 million people. Severe malnutrition left many of them too listless to learn in school if they were children, or to look for work if they were adults. I came to feel that hunger was a tragedy in a country such as India but only a scandal in the United States, where it was so preventable, so curable. The hungry can be cured simply—by food. The underclass, though, is incurable by any means yet tried. Professor William Julius Wilson of the University of Chicago, who might be called the bard of the underclass because he has written about it so extensively, dislikes the term 'underclass', which he finds denigrating though he, too, uses it. He would prefer to see the urban minority poor helped rather than blamed for their plight. Whether our fellow citizens are equated with the "old" lower class or form a "new" underclass, their numbers are growing. Wilson's most prominent antagonist on the right, sociologist Charles Murray, travels the country delivering a lecture on the underclass titled "The Case for Blaming the Victim." Yet, even if Wilson and Murray disagree on what to do about it, they agree the problem is sizable.

How sizable? Before we get to the underclass, what is the structure of poverty in general? If you go beyond the nucleus of the persistently poor, beyond the outer core of those the government labels poor, to include those who work at least part of the time but are treacherously close to poverty's precipice, you can hear the figure 75 million. That is not only the underclass or even the poor; 75 million includes those who perch just above the poor and therefore fear poverty the most. This high figure also takes in the portion of our population who need the services—every kind of medical care, police protection, education, drug counseling—that are most heavily strained by the mere existence of an underclass below them.

The federal government places the official poverty level along a sliding scale on which—in 1994—a family of four would be counted as poor if its annual earnings were less than $14,763. A smaller family would be poor on a lower income, a larger family poor on a somewhat higher one. By this standard, the U.S. Census Bureau concluded at the end of 1994 that 39.3 million Americans were poor. That is the highest number of American poor since 1961. Approximately two-thirds of the poor, or 26 million, are white, 11.2 million are black, and 6.4

million are Hispanic (those of Hispanic origin may be of any race, which is why the total exceeds 39 million), with 1.7 million scattered among Asian-American, Native American, and other groups.

Anyone can be poor, but to be in the underclass you have to be one of the trapped poor—with "no exit," to use the term preferred by existentialists, "in irons" as jailers and sailors put it, or, in the word borrowed by sociology from dentistry, "impacted." If you're in the underclass, you never go out to eat in a restaurant, buy new clothes, get new toys for your children, give an elderly parent in a nursing home a birthday present, take your kid brother to a ballgame, or help your daughter pick out a wedding dress. The underclass has to do, like all class, with privilege, power, entitlement, and access—or the lack of these. The underclass lacks them all.

The bottom line for poor people is the same as everyone else's bottom line: their income. Among the *persistently* poor—those we call the underclass—there is no assured amount of money passing through their hands. Their income may be almost nothing if they are essentially charity cases or part of a primitive barter economy. Or they may stitch together several thousand dollars a year. That is why it is so hard to pin down a number, tie a ribbon around it, and call everything inside that package the underclass. To distinguish the underclass from the poor, it is useful to think of the poor as being close to the economic bottom of American society, whereas the underclass have fallen out of the bottom and do not meaningfully participate in the economy of the United States. When they get up in the morning, there is no place they have to be. No one expects them. They forage for food or whatever else they regard as a necessity. They hang out—all day. When our teenagers hang out, we may smile nostalgically or wring our hands, but either way we know the condition is temporary. The underclass hang out most of their lives, relieved by an occasional attempt at school or a job, normally ending in failure.

As to an underclass total—those who are not only poor but persistently, irremediably poor—different researchers have different inclinations, different definitions. I have seen calculations that place their numbers as low as 800,000 (a very small estimate by my reckoning), which includes only those who are noosed into the worst neighborhoods of a few large cities. I have seen figures as high as 18 million, which is roughly equivalent to that portion of the population who require more goods and services from society than they produce.

Behavior may describe the people I went looking for more accurately than geography or income. Their class insignia may be discerned in how they live. The underclass is characterized by long-term joblessness and/or welfare dependency; unwed parenting; criminal or uncivil behavior, exhibited by traumatized drunks, drug addicts, gentle drifters, released mental patients, and violent street thugs; dropping out of school; and teenage pregnancy. By this behavioral standard, the underclass edges upward to between 12 million and 15 million.

There is one more number. The most threatening figure I heard was from Los Angeles *Times* journalist Sam Fulwood, who spent a year traveling with a colleague to study poverty in America. "It's the working poor that should scare us the most," Fulwood told me after completing his research. "They are the ones whose income places them at constant risk of falling into poverty. A divorce, loss of a job or home, illness or injury or the death of a wage earner—any of these will destroy their fragile hold on the lower rungs of respectability and plunge them into desperate poverty." Fulwood estimated the number of working *and* nonworking poor at between 70 million and 75 million. "The working poor are a far cry from the impacted underclass you hear sociologists talk about," he said, "but these are the people tough times will be toughest on."

Scrutinizing them coldly, as a numbers cruncher might, I could see that the 6 or 8 or 12 million people in the hardest core underclass will not choke our system, even though their suffering undeniably drains our society. But the 39 million below the poverty level will hurt everyone, and Fulwood's figure of between 70 million and 75 million can be asphyxiating. "When this many citizens become crippled economically," Fulwood said, "everyone else's standard of living falls because the government has to find ways of accommodating

them into its programs, and that costs money. If the federal
government decides to pay no attention, local governments have to.
Sooner or later taxes rise, services fall, production declines, and the
middle class itself is eroded. Hospitals become overcrowded, parks
and subways get dirtier and less safe, and those who are not yet poor
cannot walk their streets without fear of those who are." Seventy
million people. Seventy-five million people. This means we are not
talking only about an "economic problem." We are talking about a
nuclear attack on the fabric of our society.

A chronic condition when aggravated beyond the body's ability to
adjust to it becomes an emergency. This is the emergency that
poorness in America has become. At the bottom of this emergency
lies the underclass itself. In one sense it is prostrate, almost mori-
bund. But in the sense that it sucks away the lifeblood of the society
above it, the underclass might as well be armed with 20-megaton
warheads.

I hadn't gone far with my inquiries when I realized, just by
listening to other people's mugging and wilding and urban menace
stories, how much race has to do with our perception of the
underclass. The one aspect of my own mugging that I'd been aware
of—in addition to the .45 and the nylon stocking—was that the face
of the mugger underneath the stocking was black. Busy drumming
up support for programs to help the poor, government agencies like
to stress that two-thirds of Americans in poverty are white, fewer
than one-third black. Yes, but that two-thirds includes *all* the poor,
not only the desperately poor in the cities. The urban poor who are
packed into neighborhoods from which there is no escape are far
more than one-third black. They do not by any measurement
constitute the entire American underclass, but they set the tone for
municipal impatience, anger, and fear.

Below and outside the social structure, the urban poor are in
worse condition today than ever before simply because their neighborhoods consist of almost no one but themselves. The civil rights
legislation of the '60s in general, and open housing in particular,
made it possible at last for middle-class and steadily employed blacks

to move out of inner-city ghettos to better neighborhoods and the suburbs. With so few working professionals still around, the poorest black youth are literally left with no one to turn to.

To begin in the cradle that so few of them have, four-fifths of the babies in ghetto neighborhoods are born out of wedlock and have no one playing what the middle class accepts as a normal paternal role in their lives. American teenagers have twice the number of babies, proportionately, as English and Canadian teenagers, three times as many as the French, four times as many as the Swedish, and nine times as many as the Dutch, who have virtually universal sex education. "We have something truly new under the sun," Charles Murray declares, and very few of his conservative colleagues or his liberal adversaries would disagree. It is, however, partly the inability of the assorted experts to achieve a consensus on how to help the underclass that has produced the policy impasse within both the executive and legislative branches of the government. We have done nothing about the underclass for well over a decade, nothing resolute about poverty since the '60s.

When considering underclass life in the cities, race abides. Homicide is the leading cause of death for black men between the ages of 19 and 25. From 1987 to 1989, while the murder rate for whites was declining, the rate for nonwhites rose by 16 percent. In one Chicago neighborhood, the director of the community health center told me that 40 percent of the babies are born with what he called "cocaine involvement." There are 31.4 deaths per 1000 live births, almost 4 times the national average. Seventy-two percent of blacks born in 1967 spent at least a year on welfare before their 18th birthday. (The figure for whites is 25 percent.) "Do you have any idea what it means when three-quarters of your children are on welfare?" asks Senator Daniel Patrick Moynihan, the leading congressional expert on urban poverty, referring to the predicament of black families. "When you're on welfare, you're a pauper. Your whole life is broken up. You're dealing with brain-dead, artery-clogged bureaucracies that hate you."

Looking at hunger, my doorway into poverty in the '60s, I found

new totals for the '90s. Five and a half million American children,
both black and white, go hungry often enough and long enough to
make them diseased, according to a report from the Food Research
and Action Center in Washington. Another 6 million are considered
at risk because of nutritional deficiencies in their diets. Not counting
the adults in their families, that's 11.5 million undernourished or
malnourished American children. In 1992 Tufts University's Center
on Hunger, Poverty, and Nutrition Policy released a report detailing
three different methods it had used to calculate the number of hungry
Americans. Each of the three methods arrived at the same total: 30
million. The total in the late '60s, when I looked at hunger before,
was 10 million. That's how much improvement the improvers have
wrought, pestered by those who, like me, believe in improvability.

Then there is the question, where the underclass in concerned, of
sympathy. The continued existence of the persistently poor—they are
a growth industry—mocks us. The reality is that two generations after
the New Deal scooped up so many of the disenfranchised, one full
generation after the Great Society's war on poverty skimmed off so
many more of the victims of race prejudice and entrenched poverty,
the United States possesses an army of the underclass who have
defeated, eluded, or fallen through all the nets that were presumably
designed for their rescue. They have also defeated much of the
sympathy of the people who designate themselves as friends of the
poor. I began to think about what the requirements for my sympathy
are, what they might be in the minds of most people I know.

Remember Alfred Doolittle? The stubborn father of the upwardly
mobile Eliza Doolittle welcomed the 20th century by demonstrating
who loses when liberal intentions combine with middle-class morality to confront the poor. "Undeserving poverty is my line," Doolittle
tells Professor Higgins in Shaw's *Pygmalion*.

> What am I? I'm one of the undeserving poor: that's what I am.
> Think of what that means to a man. It means that he's up agen
> middle class morality all the time. If there's anything going, and I
> put in for a bit of it, it's always the same story: "You're undeserv-
> ing; so you can't have it." But my needs is as great as the most

deserving widow's that ever got money out of six different chari-
ties in one week for the death of the same husband. I don't need
less than a deserving man; I need more. I don't eat less hearty than
him; and I drink a lot more. I want a bit of amusement, 'cause I'm a
thinking man. I want cheerfulness and a song and a band when I
feel low. Well, they charge me just the same for everything as they
charge the deserving. What is middle class morality? Just an excuse for never giving me anything.

The aptly named Doolittle made his complaint in the first decade of
the century, and he might make it also in the last, a tribute to the
continuity of our requirements for sympathy in an era widely, if
mistakenly, assumed to have encompassed as great a firestorm of
change in our emotions as it has in our technologies.

Looking for Doolittle's successors spread out across the American
landscape, I began my search for the underclass, deceptively, at the
Waldorf Astoria. This was journalistically unsound, but it was
comfortable. I sat in the Waldorf with the underclass specialist
William Julius Wilson. We were doing an unpower breakfast about
the powerless. A moment's pause before we dove into our fresh fruit
and whole-grain cereal—a pair of healthy guys wanting to stay that
way—as we said the social conscience version of grace. Right, it was
ironic we had met at the Waldorf (where he was attending a
conference) to have a skimpy breakfast that cost $40 while we talked
about the underclass.

Questioning Professor Wilson, I wondered why an underclass
exists at all. We have our enormous, taxpaying, relatively prosperous middle class and all sorts of mechanisms, from collective bar-
gaining rights to public education to the agencies spawned by the
New Deal and its offspring, the Great Society, which are supposed to
combat and even conquer chronic poverty. Food stamps, Aid to
Families with Dependent Children (AFDC), Supplemental Security
Income (SSI), Medicaid, the Women-Infants-and-Children (WIC)
program, additional emergency aid programs run by the states—
here a net, there a net, everywhere another net.

Such programs reach some of the underclass, Professor Wilson explained, but do not lift them. When they have children, they merely swell their class further. New babies for AFDC, new school dropouts, new fodder for the drug dealers, new children to have yet more children. The problem, as Wilson perceives it, is not a helping hand but the changing economy, an economy that has been transformed from manufacturing to service industries and can no longer employ an unskilled workforce in the numbers it once did. When the urban underclass, which is the segment of the persistently poor Wilson studies, looks around, it finds itself isolated from beneficial role models and stabilizing institutions that have made successful getaways. What remains are the husks of neighborhoods, as in the South Bronx, South Central Los Angeles, or large portions of the South and West Sides of Chicago. Deep poverty is like a deep freeze, Wilson believes. "Residents of inner-city neighborhoods have no option other than to remain in their neighborhoods," he said. "Social mobility leads to geographic mobility." The underclass he scrutinizes might as well be in chains for all the mobility its members have.

Stung by my own mugging, disillusioned by the lack of progress, awed by the numbers, I began my journey. My search was propelled by even more questions now, questions that mystified me the way the stars did—both in the sky and on the screen—when I first saw them as a child. Who is really out there? If the underclass ticks away, threatening a nuclear explosion inside our culture and economy, *who* ought to do *what* about it? If we're in this much danger, all of us, from the socially lethal weapons aimed at our lifestyles and pocketbooks, is sympathy for the underclass beside the point? Can we stop the attack if we want to? Can we look away again and simply do more efficient, and invisible, maintenance of the chronically poor? Is there a point in the life of every individual at which his or her will is so completely crushed that the capacity to act on his or her own behalf is forever broken? Can the flow toward failure be stopped at this point—or even at subsequent points—with the right kind of intervention? Do we have to get rid of the underclass before they get rid of us? Do we line them up and shoot them, or can we find another way to end their underclass membership?

Far from the Waldorf, back in Los Angeles, my old hometown, I had an experience on East Seventh Street that proclaims the quest at the heart of this book. Darkness was advancing over the blocks of low-slung, rickety buildings, sidewalks with broken bus stop benches, pawnshop windows, and storefronts of marginal enterprises that cashed checks or sold lottery tickets or sometimes found jobs for the poor. An exotic woman named Sherry Lane was jangling her gold bracelets with the snake's head charm in my direction. She had peroxided blonde hair and mocha skin. A long, low-slung jaw gave her a visage of moderate authority, belying the rest of her presentation, as though she might be an account executive or the chief aide to a Senate subcommittee investigating the profession she herself actually practiced. She told me proudly that even though she's losing customers to the unemployment sweeping the neighborhood her second snowbaby is now out of his incubator at County General and she is planning to see him this Saturday, Sunday for sure. "Truckers and loaders ain't working, I ain't working, honey, simple as that."

A man in a fatigue jacket shambled by, calling her over to the door of a locked and gated pawnshop. "Hey baby, wiggle up close." In one of his ears was an earring, in the other a Walkman headphone. He whispered to Sherry Lane. Between her black leather miniskirt and her tanktop was a wide silver belt. Even 20 feet away her fragrance was overpoweringly sweet, like a rain forest reeking of growth and decay, where it is spring and fall at the same time. The man in the fatigue jacket was sizing me up, and I wondered if he was giving her advice on how much to charge me.

Her slender knees poking six inches or so below her skirt as she walked, Sherry Lane returned on spiky heels to give me the news. "Sugar, my man's telling me they convicted the black dude that beat up the white trucker after the King thing. You wanna see the sun come up in the morning, you get your mama's boy's white ass back over to the West Side where it belongs. Fourth a Jew-lie's gonna start up downtown tonight, white man in a tie don't wanna be down here lookin' for no black nooky. You shut your questions I spot you a blow job send you on your way."

She was referring to the trial of the black defendants who had attacked a white truck driver in the furious reaction after four Los Angeles policemen had been acquitted of brutality in the beating of Rodney King that the whole world had seen on an accidental videotape. The Los Angeles riot, like the earthquake two years later, changed the way the city thought about itself. I watched Sherry Lane evaporate into the murk of East Seventh Street with her pimp and then, taking her suggestion, I, too, evaporated onto the Santa Monica Freeway.

Sherry Lane's gifts included a talent for summary. Those who usually buy what the persistently poor have to sell, physical labor of one kind or another, were themselves working only sporadically. Hard times make the poorest even poorer, and they are already isolated not only socially but geographically from the rest of the citizenry. She was even right about my own locale and direction. We were in the city where I grew up, I was headed for its West Side, and I was indeed going to have dinner with my mother.

As it turned out, there was no riot in Los Angeles after the conclusion of the trial that Sherry Lane had announced as clearly as if she were a CNN anchor. The convictions obtained in the beating of the truck driver were on lesser charges than the defendants had been accused of, and by that time there had already been a second trial in the Rodney King beating, in which two of the policemen had been convicted. But Sherry Lane had a good memory and an affable pimp, both of them considerate of the danger a potential white customer would face in any outbreak of racial violence. The fact that there was no new Los Angeles riot that night, or that my interest in Sherry Lane was not in pursuit of her profession but my own, only illuminated the chasm between us: a writer in search of his subject, a whore in search of business not so she can support her children, who in any case have been taken from her, but her coke habit. Old enough to have grown up in the fractious '60s, young enough still to be doing a brisk street trade when the economy permits, Sherry Lane is living by rumor and the whiff of trouble. When she received both from her pimp, who has the kind of credibility with Sherry Lane that a priest has with a

Mediterranean fishwife, she kindly warned off a white questioner and went on with her evening's rounds in her hometown and mine.

The poorest poor have offered me intimate details of their lives. I have found them open and trusting. They have told me about their families, their sex lives, the amount of money they have, their drug use, their fears for their children. Some were no doubt glad of the temporary attention, but by far the greater number expressed the hope that by committing their stories to general scrutiny, they would be putting the problems of the underclass before a potentially responsive public. In return for their help, I have felt that both truth and privacy can best be served by changing their names. As to the accuracy of their testimony, my sense is that I was generally listening to details no one but a novelist could make up and that when I heard wishes and fears along with facts, these were completely authentic in terms of the perceptions of the person talking to me. In addition to listening to them, I have also observed them; they live as they speak. If you have ever interviewed politicians, executives, or entertainers, I'm not sure you found them nearly as credible in the matter of accuracy, and no doubt they were a great deal more buttressed and defended than the persistently poor. My encounter with Sherry Lane was typical. She presented and represented herself, no one else.

I found myself in a dark thicket when I began to consider the poorest poor. This was not only because they themselves are such an intractable part of society, not only because, suffering, they at first made me reflexively turn away, but because they are such a problem even semantically—who and where they are, which ones are sick, which addicted, which young, which black, and on and on—I could not even rub two specialists together who agreed on their identity. That is why I was grateful to meet Sherry Lane and her pimp, along with everyone else I am about to introduce you to.

Back and forth between the rigorous Northeast and the easeful Sunbelt, I wanted to put faces on the figures I had compiled. I decided to follow the underclass from infancy to old age. This would bring me to the deepest poor in the varieties of their experience, united in a common condition wherever I went: Chicago, Los Angeles, Oakland, San Antonio, and the area around Bangor, Maine. Each place, each stage of life, left me perplexed and informed by what I saw, yet never without reeling, when I recalled the picture the republic has of itself, at the coexistence of our soaring riches and infernal destitution. The persistently poor are persistently with us. The same America that nourishes my family, and yours, crushes theirs.

3
Babies and Children

Born There

"Back when I didn't know I could charge for it," Sherry Lane told me before her pimp gave her the report on the trial results that sent each of us scurrying from the other, "I gave away, oh, at least a million dollars' worth of the stuff." She seemed neither regretful nor boastful as she told me this, merely factual, knitting her brows when she made her million-dollar estimate. There was a toughness to Sherry Lane that turned away pity. I thought she might be a female version of my mugger.

I found myself speculating, as I had about the mugger, what circumstances would have to occur to bring me to a point where I'd first give my body to anyone who wanted it, which Sherry Lane indicated she had, then stop giving it and start selling it. Much later, in Chicago, I met some teenagers who were Sherry Lanes-in-the-making, and then I understood more. For now, I had to invent a whole new childhood for myself. It was less difficult to imagine myself born a girl than to invent memories of being alternately beaten and ignored as a child, later raped by a boyfriend of my mother, still later thrown out of a smelly apartment that had only one unbroken window. At that point I gave up. I realized Sherry Lane had a background so alien to mine that any attempt I might make either to identify with her or impose my values on her was doomed to failure.

What Sherry Lane did not give away was her first snowbaby. She sold him. She named him Tresor Le after a pop singer she liked, and he stayed in an incubator over a month because he was delivered at 29 weeks and weighed two pounds. The only glimpse Sherry Lane may have given me into her psyche was that she blinked her artificial lashes rapidly as she told me she sold Tresor Le to her coke dealer. Surely she was not blinking back tears. Crying was as foreign to Sherry Lane as middle-class guilt. Still, she could feel, and express, pain. I thought perhaps there was pain in her blinking—pain for her lost baby, for herself, for the impossible distance between where she was and any more favorable circumstance. She fingered the snake's head charm on her bracelet as she told me about Tresor Le, her extralong fingernails clicking against the bracelet's links. But our talk had been curtailed by the arrival of her pimp.

I learned a few more details about Sherry Lane and Tresor Le when I returned a few days later to East Seventh Street. Another woman, describing herself as a retired prostitute who now does social work in the neighborhood (an assertion I did not take too seriously), said her friend Sherry Lane was "temporarily out of commission." I was unable to find out whether that meant sick, arrested, in a crack house, or some other misfortune that would keep her off the job. But the woman did seem to know Sherry Lane well.

At Country General Hospital, my new informant said, Sherry Lane's first baby soon reached four pounds, twice his birth weight, indicating that she and Sherry Lane were at least talking about the same baby. The nurses in the neonatal intensive care unit noticed that he quivered sometimes. At five pounds Tresor Le became irritable. When his eyes opened he couldn't maintain contact. The doctor said Tresor Le's system had undergone damage *in utero* due to his mother's cocaine habit. Finally, Sherry Lane took Tresor Le home. That was when she sold him to her dealer for a week's worth of half-grams, which normally cost her between $400 and $500. The dealer had a touch of kindness and took the baby to Tresor Le's grandmother, the father's mother, and told her what Sherry Lane had done. The grandmother kept Tresor Le for three weeks but he

was too agitated for her—"He's bouncing off the walls," she said—
and so she turned him over to the Department of Human Services,
which hoped to find him a foster home someday. Those were the first
weeks in the life of Tresor Le. Sherry Lane's friend said Tresor Le was
now over a year old and had disappeared into the welfare system.
She'd heard that, to make him more adoptable, Tresor Le had been
given a new name.

I remembered Sherry Lane saying she had a second child, also
described as a snowbaby because of the mother's cocaine addiction.
In the infants' ward at County General I was turned away by a
Belgian doctor who told me firmly that the right to privacy begins at
birth, so I could not see any of the babies in the ward. She added
helpfully, however, that the babies from cocaine- and crack-addicted
mothers were subject to the same withdrawal symptoms adults
would have if they abruptly gave up drug habits. She had seen babies
shake uncontrollably, lose weight, be unable to sleep, and have the
type of seizures associated with epilepsy. I asked whether, to alleviate
withdrawal symptoms, the babies were treated with small doses of
their mothers' habitual drugs. She said no, they were treated with
sedatives that would modify their withdrawal syndromes and mini-
mize seizures. Some of the babies became normal after several
months. Others had developmental difficulties that would last for
years. Some were permanently retarded.

A second, nocturnal visit to County General was a little more
productive. A nurse's aide in the infants' ward knew the baby when I
gave his mother's name, profession, and a description of her as an
addict. She could not let me see Sherry Lane's second snowbaby; she
said he was having problems but would probably be okay. His
mother had not returned to see him since leaving the hospital two
days after giving birth.

Discouraged, I turned to leave the ward. Just then a baby was
being moved somewhere, wheeled along in a tray with transparent
sides by another nurse's aide. The corridor was dimly lighted and I
was unable to catch the name tag on the tray. I asked the aide I'd been
speaking to if this was one of the cocaine babies. She said, "No, well,

yes." I asked if it happened to be Sherry Lane's, and she shut up entirely. She knew, I gathered, that she should be kicking me out of there, but I thought she was a little intimidated by my tie and, oddly, my height which, even well under six feet, was considerably to the north of her own. The baby, sleeping peacefully in his tray, was a fair-skinned infant with a strong jaw like Sherry Lane's. I watched the baby sleep, grateful not to have to see any twitching. As the two nurse's aides chatted and I was figuring out how best to make my retreat, the infant stiffened and then began to shiver in a way I've never seen in any of my own four children. Swathed in blankets, he was clearly not cold. The shivering continued perhaps 30 endless seconds. The nurse's aides barely glanced at the tray. This was not unusual behavior to them. The shivering reached a convulsing crescendo, then slowly subsided. Even in his sleep, I thought. As soon as he stopped shivering I turned away and left, feeling useless.

From birth, a kneebone-connected-to-the-thighbone poverty skeleton emerges among underclass babies like Sherry Lane's. The simple learning experiences of childhood are possessed by anguish and surrender. If you are an unfed, untended, or abused child, you cannot develop your abilities. If you cannot develop along with your age group, you won't be able to study properly in the classroom. If you can't study, you can't finish school. If you can't finish school, you can't get a good job. If you can't get a good job, you can't fit into the economy. If you can't fit into the economy in a constructive way, you become a destructive element who subtracts from rather than adds to the common weal. These are the lineaments of the lives of the persistently poor. Their early failures are accompanied by the failure of those above them, like me, to appreciate how improbable it is that they will pull themselves out of such backgrounds.

"Quit fiddlefucking with my hair, goddamn ya Frito, before I lay you out!" This is what five-year-old Frito often hears from her mother Carlotta D'Souza, a woman of supple contradiction, and these are the words I heard her say several times in the downtown Los Angeles soup kitchen where I met her. Carlotta has kindly eyes, but speaks harshly and mostly refuses to smile. I saw her laugh only once, furtively, at a remark made by a man she was with who seemed younger and was not Frito's father. Her brief smile revealed front teeth that were discolored, almost black. I had gone to the soup kitchen after three skid row winos, seated on the sidewalk sunning themselves against a graffiti-covered brick wall as they shared a half gallon jug among them, recommended it almost wholeheartedly. "Two and a half stars, Champ," one of them said as I moved off in the direction they pointed.

The soup kitchen is in the dining room of the Midnight Mission, huge and clean and recently painted when I was there, but inauspiciously quiet. "In and out, in and out," the manager of the kitchen told me. "We run it like a military operation. No smoking, no loud talking. We can feed 100 at a time, 1,600 a day." Yellow ceilings, white chairs, lime green walls, orange tables, tables and chairs anchored to the floors, as in a McDonald's. It was not homey, but it got the job done. Sixteen hundred a day, as the manager said.

I was drawn to Frito because of her bounce. Perhaps 90 people the manager described as "mostly regulars" were eating glumly, wordlessly. I felt sorry for them, but I found their looks of depression depressing, and at this early stage of my journey I avoided them. Frito, by contrast, was all over the room, pulling at the beard of an ancient Mexican at the next table, which made him laugh, and making a teepee out of the stringbeans of a bag lady with no teeth. The lady tousled Frito's hair, but Carlotta was annoyed at the behavior strangers found amusing.

Frito has her mother's green eyes and sandy curls, the curls Carlotta warned her to stop playing with. That day Frito also had a cut on her chin, which she said she got from a potato peeler she was trying to learn to use. She likes to laugh and get into everything, the kitchen manager told me, while her mother stays moody and quiet. Many of the regulars recognized Frito at the mission, as well as Carlotta and Carlotta's boyfriend Ridley, who was friendly with everyone, especially with Frito. The ties between the kitchen regulars seemed loose. They tended to gather in clusters and there wasn't much communication between the clusters. Frito, however, hopped around like a sprite. Each cluster looked up to smile at her. The Midnight Mission now pulls in more blacks and Hispanics than whites, and Frito's little family is white. Ridley is from northern Indiana, Carlotta is an exotic amalgam of Maltese and Portuguese, and Frito's disappeared father is Welsh.

I had planned to mingle with different clusters but found myself more comfortable eating with Frito's family who were, as I found when I did venture to a couple of nearby groups, more communicative than the others. This was my third soup kitchen, and I was finding people easier to approach when I had my own lunch tray. The food was big-kitchen generic—boiled carrots, macaroni and cheese, fried drumsticks—and I've blundered into it, with small variation, at institutions ranging from prisons to parochial schools. When Frito returned from playing with a group of older men, Carlotta greeted her with a disapproving frown that Ridley mocked by pretending to be serious with Frito. Carlotta glared at Ridley, then lit a cigarette that she was only two drags into before an attendant asked her to wait until she was outside to smoke. Whatever other social neglect is visited on them, members of the underclass are included in the national instructions to maintain healthy lungs.

After the threat that she'd be hit if she didn't take her hands off her mother's hair, Frito, who had been playing with everyone walking by, was silent. She picked at her macaroni until lunch was over. Outside the soup kitchen, her mother and Ridley looked for a man who had been around earlier with the promise of day work. Carlotta searched anxiously for the man, almost desperately, but Ridley was casual. This was similar to the way they treated Frito: Ridley was easy with her, Carlotta bore down hard on her only child. Sidling in my direction, Frito shared an anxiety with me in the uninhibited way small children have of communicating personally with strangers, yielding up pieces of their lives.

"I don't like my mom's black teeth," she said. "That's why she don't smile; she don't want anyone to see them." Frito told me her mother was riding in a pickup truck near Fresno, where she had gone to pick tomatoes, when the truck ran off the road. It hit a telephone pole and Carlotta was smashed in the mouth. "I like my mother to have pretty teeth like she did before," Frito said, "so if we make some money she's going to get her black teeth white again. Can they make black teeth white?"

Wherever I went among the underclass, a detail such as Carlotta's blackened teeth represented a whole set of problems. These involved health, embarrassment, the difficulty of being well-groomed, and, as always, money. Though they are without cash for decent clothes or haircuts, not to mention dentistry, the persistently poor can be as self-conscious as the middle class about their appearance. After years without hope of changing their appearance, they become accustomed to looking poor, but they are never in doubt that they *do* look poor, and poorly.

Worrying about her mother's teeth, Frito at the age of five was already aware of broader standards outside her family. When she told me about Carlotta's teeth, I wanted at first to distract Frito with something pleasant, a game maybe, the equivalent of saying, Oh Frito, it really doesn't matter as long as she's your mom and she loves you. The trouble was, Frito's mother's love was itself in a dubious part of the emotional forest, and the little girl's eyes were imploring me to pay attention to what she was saying, so I did. Probably it was only myself whom I wanted to distract. "Dentists have these things called caps," I told Frito, "and they put them on your teeth, and the caps make your teeth white as snow." Then I wondered whether the little southern California girl even knew what snow is; I myself certainly hadn't at her age. And, of course, "they" don't give caps away. Carlotta's problem is endemic to the underclass: You don't have enough money to make yourself look acceptable, so you're not accepted into a job where you could get the money to make yourself look acceptable.

No one ever calls Frito anything but Frito, including her mother and Ridley, but it is not her name. Carlotta named her daughter Gelisse, after a Portuguese grandmother, but people didn't say it right, so an aunt began calling her Frito after a junk food she teethed on as a baby. "Our people came from Cape St. Vincent and Setubal originally," Carlotta told me after she and Ridley had given up looking for the man who had promised a day's work. "In the 19th century we had boats. Made a good living that way. Proud fisherfolk, you know." She allowed herself a quick smile when she said the word "fisherfolk," a flashback to a time she'd only heard of but treasured possessively. She returned ruefully to the present. "Ridley don't understand the girl even if he's nicer to her than I am, I'll admit it. The only way to get her to mind is a swat. He just makes dolls for Frito out of old rubber balls and twine and thumbtacks."

Despite Frito's cheerfulness, she gives the impression of tagging along. She and her mother have lived seven places in the past year. Above a pawnshop, in a shelter, below a street-level butcher shop, in a Kern County migrant's shack, in a shelter again, and so on. They receive no welfare. Carlotta, Frito and Ridley each offered me different slices of their lives. Frito told me Ridley is mostly with them, which she likes because Carlotta gets more moody when Ridley is gone. Frito does know her father, Ridley told me, but her father hits her mother worse than her mother hits Frito. Carlotta told me she was going to get a court order against Frito's father to prevent him from coming around. "Guy wants custody. Him! He should have custody of a pit bull." Given to drinking, fighting, and occasional small burglaries, Frito's father was currently in jail, a relief to Carlotta. "I fell for him big time. Plans, he was full of plans. We was going to run a coffee shop; he's Greek on his mother's side. Guy couldn't stay sober long enough to eat a sandwich, never mind make one."

Ridley, not particularly focused on anything farther away than the end of the week, manages to play a part in Frito's life, combining aspects of a young uncle and a much older brother. He accepts Frito uncritically, showing interest in her games because he is still something of a kid himself. He lets Frito climb all over him, and he doesn't swat her off the way Carlotta does. When I saw them another time at the soup kitchen, Ridley was standing in line for food and Frito was climbing up his pants to his waist. Then she grabbed his arm as if it were a branch on a tree and hoisted herself up onto his shoulders. "I'm your jungle gym, huh Frito," Ridley said affection-ately. After Frito slid down Ridley's torso, she pinched him on his blue-jeaned butt, and Ridley laughed and hugged her.

Ridley is only 20, six years younger than Frito's mother. The afternoon I spent with them, Ridley could almost have been Frito's playmate. Yet he had an easy, sophisticated attitude about Carlotta, extending even to her own childhood, which, of course, he can only have heard about from her. He told me Carlotta can be cheerful enough until she starts fretting about her five-year-old. "When she gets nervous she gets, like, her daughter and her mother at the same time. What she's told me about her mother anyway. Her mom would whack Carlotta for asking, you know, if she could have a piece of toast." Because I had already met a number of young underclass mothers with children they don't take care of very well, I felt I was seeing a pattern. Coming out of unstable backgrounds, they find men—or are found by them—who seem to promise improvement but aren't able to deliver. Trying to repair their own pasts, these young mothers end up repeating them. This pattern, obviously, is hardly confined to a single social class, but it is the poor who are economically trapped in their patterns; the better off among us may find ourselves emotionally trapped, but we will still send our children to college. "It happens before she knows it when she gets pee-ohed," Ridley said. "Suddenly Carlotta's smacking Frito around like her mother did her."

As we strolled through skid row catching the last of the winter sun over downtown Los Angeles, Frito and Ridley described their recent history to me. I was getting to know this little family, and they in turn acted as though they were comfortable with me. Even Carlotta relaxed and seemed glad to be with a stranger who was curious about her life. I was as charmed by Frito as I was worried for her. I was interested in Ridley, who I thought would move on someday just because he liked to wander, and I was anxious about Carlotta because she seemed to live her life pursued by a cloud. For a while in the fall, she'd had a job in a diner in Monrovia, east of Los Angeles, and Frito had gone to kindergarten.

Working nights, Carlotta told me, she hadn't gotten Frito to the kindergarten on time more than twice during the first four weeks. Then Ridley came back from a construction job near San Bernardino, and he had Frito at school by 7:45 A.M. three days in a row, but at the end of the third day Frito pushed a little boy into a swing that someone else was already swinging in. The boy lost his two front teeth. They were only his baby teeth, but the boy's mother complained that too much of "the element" was finding its way into their neighborhood school. If you had to have rough stuff in kindergarten, where could you go to grow up gentle?

The kindergarten teacher told Carlotta she thought Frito should stay home for a while—"home" currently being a one-room apartment above a veterinarian's office. Although this latest lodging was sounding like a Dickensian cliché, Ridley brought the squalid scene to life (as Dickens might have) by recalling the conversation after Frito's expulsion from kindergarten. "I've had it with this brat," Carlotta had told Ridley that night over the din of the yelping dogs and howling cats downstairs. "She cleans up her act or she goes to a foster home." Frito said she was only joking with the little boy.

Yet Carlotta was not so heartless. She was not simply an impaired mother. She confessed to me she knew she was not giving her daughter the childhood she deserved. "All's I'm giving Frito is what I had myself," she told me as Ridley and Frito jumped over a fire hydrant ahead of us. "What good is that? Poor little girl needs more and oughta get more, and I ain't giving it to her. Maybe somebody else would." I looked at her to see if she meant that, and she went on. "Yet she's all I have, isn't she? I mean Ridley, I got Ridley, but he's liable to split one of these days. So what I got is Frito, and what she's got is me."

We reached a corner where a young man in a tanktop, with a red bandana around his shaved head, had just vacated a metal folding chair to push a shopping cart down the sidewalk. The shopping cart was filled with empty cans he had collected off the street. Like several other men around the neighborhood with much time and modest enterprise, he was pushing his load toward a recycling depot where he could get a nickel a can. Since the cleanup and restoration of Pershing Square in the heart of downtown, the poor have taken to gathering elsewhere, and the metal folding chairs now appear on street corners. The three winos who had directed me to the Midnight Mission would once have been found in Pershing Square, and Frito's family might have spent the afternoon there. The square is now not only renovated but also patroled. A positive gain for the downtown business class becomes another loss for the underclass. But the shopping cart man in the tanktop did leave behind an empty chair on a sunny corner. Carlotta settled herself into it while Frito and Ridley buzzed around her. Frito asked her mother when she could go to school again. "We're looking at a whole boxcar of things to think about besides you going to school," Carlotta said, "and anyway, you messed up bad the last time."

Frito looked up at Ridley to see if he would give her a different answer. Ridley had started a conversation with a tow-haired young man about a meat-packing job. They seemed to know each other slightly. "What you have to do," the young man was telling Ridley, "is you have to get you a sweater to last it our in the refrigeration room." The man took a pull on a bottle of beer he had in a paper bag. Frito finally got Ridley's attention and asked him about school. "You play the hand you're dealt," Ridley said, winking down at her, "but if it wasn't for bad luck, Frito, you wouldn't have no luck at all."

What part of some larger social picture was Frito's family a detail in? They discouraged me, Carlotta and Ridley and Frito. It was not that economic gains were the only benefits and that these were being denied to this trio. It was more a matter of ground. There was simply no ground beneath their feet, nor much air for them to breathe. They might have been floating in outer space. Carlotta would float toward some other attachment after Ridley floated off. Frito, plucky if not lucky, might stay unpregnant when she hit the teenage years, but she would not find a school that could hold her, she wouldn't acquire a skill that could sustain her, and eventually, she, too, would float off into some dead-end corner of space that would remain, for all the promise I could detect, the black hole of the underclass.

My journey to the children of the persistently poor could easily have begun and ended in Los Angeles, where I grew up protected from them. Surely I could find more deprived children there than I could handle. But even as a native, I didn't quite trust Los Angeles any more than outsiders do. Staying in Los Angeles, I wouldn't know enough about the national vista and would principally be adding irony to my own memory. For those who don't live there, LA is its own special LA self. Its data don't travel well, and its social price tags carry a credibility discount. So I left.

From Los Angeles I went to San Antonio, a center of Spanish-American culture that now has an Hispanic majority. It appears a graceful city bisected by a gentle, meandering river. Along the San Antonio River the city fathers have planted a cobblestone walkway to give visitors a glimpse into a romantic past—or at least into a romanticized version of the past that also includes, of course, the Alamo carnage celebrated a few blocks away. In the fashion of the rest of the country, San Antonio is uplinked to its suburbs by the freeways that enable us to pass from our offices to our homes without seeing what lies underneath the elevated concrete ribbons. Underneath is the underclass. One-third of the city's children live in poverty. In the barrios of San Antonio the conditions, and the customs they lead to, are unique and yet bear a family resemblance to those Tresor Le and Frito are growing up with in Los Angeles. Texas and its immigrants, the United States and Mexico, urban renewal and poverty, all merge in San Antonio.

Children in the decaying San Antonio projects begin sniffing whatever makes them feel better at the age of nine. This is described in the social service agencies as inhalant abuse and includes aerosol products, paint, glue, Freon, antifreeze, hair spray, nail-polish remover, gasoline, Wite-Out, and felt-tipped pens. There is no way to keep children away from all these products, most of which are ordinary household items. By the time they are 12, the children are addicts, often known as sprayheads because of the kinds of drugs they take. Drugs are in every neighborhood in every city, but I found more of a narcotic shopping bazaar in San Antonio than elsewhere. According to social workers I spoke to, this is due partly to the lack of cash among kids in the barrio, which spurs creativity in the choice of consumer products that contain mood-altering chemicals, and partly due to the absence of big-city drug syndicates with the sophisticated marketing techniques found elsewhere.

I wanted to see how the youngsters who elude supervision fill their time. Just before noon on a schoolday, I watched three young boys leave a hardware store carrying a can of spray paint wrapped in a raincoat. My Spanish is awful, so I tried a simple "Hi, what's happening?" They were startled at first, but they spoke English, which I later discovered is not the case with all San Antonio children. After walking with them back toward their housing project and assuring them I was neither a policeman nor a truant officer, I asked how old they were. One of the sprayheads said they were 10.

The boys all had stringy brown hair. The one who said they were 10 had large eyes that seemed still to be trusting. Another had a scar beneath one ear, and the nose of the third was crooked from being broken, he said, by his uncle. The boy with large eyes said the uncle of the crooked-nosed boy wasn't really an uncle but someone who visited his mother. They boy with the crooked nose shrugged in confirmation. The boys knew their neighborhood well, scurrying through it as familiarly as if they were twice their ages, yet they impressed me as quite lost. None had any plans or anyone helping him make plans. Only one of them knew where either of his parents was. "My mother's at the food stamp place," the boy with the scar said. His scar started underneath his earlobe and traveled to the back of his neck, where it stopped in a small lump of whitish flesh. Where the lump grew, hair did not.

I asked when was the last time they had been in school. The 10-year-old with the large eyes said he didn't go anymore. The boy with the broken nose said he was going to go next week but wasn't sure when he had last gone. The boy with the scar beneath his ear said he had gone the week before and was going to go the following day. "I'm taking a little day off; my oldest sister said it was okay because I did her a big favor yesterday." The favor, he explained, was to keep a secret from their mother about where she had gone on the weekend. He gave no more details, leaving me to surmise a trip across the border or to a borrowed apartment with a boyfriend or a secret abortion. The boy shut up completely when I asked how he got his scar. The boy with the large eyes said only, "His grandfather."

I would not characterize these children as aimless. They were full of small purposes and temporary directions. But their aims were those that will keep them in this barrio until they are carried out of it, back to Mexico to be buried with their ancestors.

Few social problems are so in need of solution as extreme poverty in childhood, if only because of all the other problems it gives rise to. I wondered what was going on in the community that might offer a different future to these three boys. If their families were not able to support their growth toward fruitful membership in society, was anything else? In San Antonio's west side barrio, I visited three exceptional agencies that try to give families a chance not only to break the grip of inhalant abuse on their children but to strive toward a degree of self-reliance they have never had.

The Inman Christian Center is a comprehensive day-care facility serving low-income and welfare families. In addition to combating substance abuse, Inman's directors, Dan and Judy Saucedo, run programs in early childhood education, health care, and therapeutic services. The Saucedos are middle-aged enthusiasts, unsurrendering believers in the potential of their neighbors and their neighborhood. Dan Saucedo, having grown up in the '50s and now in his 50s, recalled the transformation of housing projects, such as his barrio's Alazan Apache Courts, from one generation's solution into the next generation's problem. The progressive, low-slung buildings of the late '40s, when postwar prosperity decreed modern architecture into city slums, now seem quaintly anachronistic at best, mere warehouses for hiding poverty at worst. "Those of us growing up in this neighborhood envied the families that could move into Alazan Apache," Dan Saucedo told me. "They had running water and noisy commodes, we had privies. Over time, the commodes broke and weren't fixed, vandals and pushers moved in, everything started to leak, and the image was gone. Now you have a stigma if you live in the Courts."

The Inman Center runs a treatment residence outside San Antonio for young addicts. Though the facility can house only a dozen at a time, the children are supposed to stay a year, long enough to break their habits, if they're motivated, in a setting remote from the projects. The problem, Judy Saucedo told me, is what happens after the year is over. "They come right back into the projects where they got the addiction in the first place." The need, as Judy Saucedo summarized it and I saw myself, is for earlier intervention, significantly more treatment centers than are now available, and an aftercare program that presents children with other kinds of stimulation and excitement besides drug addiction.

A second agency, Avancé, is an ambitious and well known organization that helps children and parents—mostly mothers because very few fathers show up—at the same time. With one-third of San Antonio's children living in poverty, Avancé and other local agencies have a fertile territory for their efforts. In the toddler group that I observed, the caregiving was intuitive, direct, and virtually parental. Teachers and assistants played on the floor with the infants, tumbling with them, showing them how to build blocks, helping them walk. The children seemed as comfortable with their teachers as with their mothers, who were also present. Two little girls in the group I watched toddled into each other and fell down. Both cried. One toddled right over to her mother for comfort, the other sobbed into her teacher's bosom.

Avancé programs begin in the cradle and proceed through all aspects of child development. Like the Inman Center, Avancé receives a combination of public and private funding, mostly federal money that passes through state and city governments. Avancé and the Inman Center provide similar kinds of services to children and their parents, but they can hardly be said to duplicate one another because the needs they address are so much greater than the help they are able to give. Good people doing good things, I felt as I watched the Avancé childhood program, shouldn't be presented as an excuse for not looking at the larger issue. The larger issue is that the numbers of the chronically poor—and their children—so over-balance the services available to them as to render agencies like the Inman Center and Avancé mere whistles in the dark.

The third agency I visited, a bilingual project known as Our Casas, promotes independence among residents of public housing. Unlike Avancé and Inman, Our Casas concentrates on housing itself. Tenants are encouraged to serve on housing project boards of directors, as well as to hire their own building managers, mainte-nance staff, and repair workers. "Our mission is collective owner-ship," Dario Chapa, Our Casas' director, told me. "To that end, we organize and train people to take over the management of their own housing projects and everything else that leads to self-sufficiency. We manage and start up our own economic development." In Our Casas, which expresses the ideals of its early supporter, former Health and Human Services Secretary Jack Kemp, the hope is that children will grow up in an atmosphere of self-reliance rather than the vassalage of welfare dependency.

A range of issues was coming into view for me. The bilingualism in Our Casas is an admirable attempt at merging cultures, but it is also, like the project itself, neither the "here" of English nor the "allá" of Spanish. The project intends people to own their homes, a classic American article of faith. Yet the concept of ownership be-comes murky when what you own is a wreck, as I soon discovered to be the case with much of the public housing I visited. Aspirations of sponsors like Jack Kemp, and later Bill Clinton, quickly conflict with a reality in which a third-generation poverty family finds itself the proprietor of a dump. It is not as though, for instance, you can repair a couple of plumbing leaks, scatter some fresh grass seed, put up vinyl siding, and sell the place for a profit, the way you might in Scarsdale or Encino. Was somebody trying to throw a saddle meant for a horse over the mountainous hump of a camel?

I was wrestling toward a judgment that a middle-class sacrament
—home ownership—is being imposed stubbornly on an underclass
for whom such a communion must turn to ashes. It seems fairly
obvious that ownership becomes a worthy goal only when you have
something worth owning. Projects only 30 or 40 years old look
worse, more dilapidated, than ancient ruins. What's to own? When it
cut funds for new public housing and proposed a tax on housing assistance, the Clinton administration showed every sign of continuing
the blinkered approach of treating the poor as though they possessed
the resources, materially and culturally, of the unpoor.

If Dario Chapa, the director of Our Casas, entertains such doubts,
he does not express them. He eagerly touts his project's goal of
having the poor take ownership of, and responsibility for, their
dwellings. Dario Chapa's enthusiasm is, I can't deny it, infectious.
He is a buoyant man who is able to lend his buoyancy to others
without losing it himself. Through his initiatives, Our Casas gives
families a chance to participate in the management of their homes for
the first time. There is always the possibility that the fact of
possession, all by itself, is better than the fact of dispossession. When
a 20-year-old mother of four came into Chapa's office, discouraged
that her toilet and sink had not worked in six weeks, Chapa pepped
her up by sending an assistant with her to confront the building
superintendent on the spot. That part of Our Casas' mission—
advocacy for the tenants—was an unambiguous success.

The complaints I heard in the neighborhood had to do with the
physical plants Our Casas has to work with. Everyone in the
neighborhood praised the aim of self-reliance. But it wasn't clear to
me that getting tenants to manage a broken-down project such as the
Alazan Apache Courts is much more of a morale builder than
turning prison cells over to their inmates. There is still no escape. In
addition, once they own the Alazan Apache, what happens when the
housing deteriorates even further? Whom then do the poorest poor
turn to, without even an apathetic public agency to spindle their
complaints? They are left to stew in their own juices while the rest of
us sagely shake our heads and say, "Look it's their own fault; the

place is all theirs and they turn it into a pigsty." The only way I saw for Our Casas to prove beneficial in the long run is if other problems of the persistently poor are also addressed at the same time. Commitments to decent housing, improved education, family planning and stability, job training, and cultural integration could make Our Casas' goal of home ownership meaningful. But in the short run—and politicians get elected and reelected in the short run—these commitments are costly without showing either financial or electoral returns. They are not much closer to being national priorities than is the establishment of a Tibetan lamasery in Wyoming.

Touring Alazan Apache with a colleague of Dario Chapa, I saw how much more would be required for repair and reconstruction than the almost nonexistent resources of project residents. Social service bureaucracies, such as the Housing Authority and welfare agencies, can frustrate the designs of Our Casas. The accumulated welfare rules decree fatherlessness in a way I was about to see, and Alazan Apache residents firmly maintain that the Housing Authority prizes regulation over renovation. Institutional neglect was visible everywhere. Walls have holes in them big enough for a child to ride a tricycle through. Plumbing and electrical systems have been vandalized for copper tubing and workable fixtures. Broken windows are boarded rather than reglazed. Windows become walls and walls become windows.

The officials in charge of relief often provide little more than a new level of harassment. "The minute you report any wages," an angry and articulate 28-year-old mother of three told me, "you're finished." Her eyes flashing, this woman told me to write down her name—Alicia—and said I should listen up because she was only going to say this once. She ran up to me, sinewy and angular as a dancer, while I was leaving one ramshackle tenement and heading toward another. A neighbor had told her than an Anglo was touring the Courts. Whether she saw me as a sympathetic official or a hostile intruder, she reported her grievances directly and succinctly. Alicia has the high cheekbones and open features of Mexicans with mixed

Spanish and Indian ancestry—Mestizos—and her English was, for this section of San Antonio, remarkable. "You report wages, your rent goes from zero to half your income," Alicia said. "That rule also breaks up households. If your man is in the house, the welfare stops paying. Men who make a little money but can't find regular work, they leave rather than see their kids thrown off welfare and force their families' rents up. So your kids lose their father and sit in front of the TV feeling like they forced him out since they know it's their presence that proves his existence." In this single stroke Alicia summarized her own predicament and indicted the system that kept her in it. "The welfare tells me to get a job, I tell them to show me where I can get one and still be a mother. The politicians tell me to be patient, I tell them to be human. Help me or don't preach to me!" By now Alicia was yelling. She ran off to pick up her baby, who had been watched for the day by another woman while Alicia took a bus downtown to look for work as a waitress. Though she had no time for further discussion and was not in a discussing mood anyway, I was cheered, perhaps perversely, by the meeting with Alicia. She was mad, she knew what she was up against, and she hadn't capitulated.

Next, I met a little boy playing on a broken swing in a littered yard while his mother watched him. At five, Miguel Espinosa is the youngest of four children, and he has never been healthy. He has weak legs, looks malnourished, and is not in any educational or child development program. Miguel is no immigrant—his mother Mercedes has lived in the Alazan Apache Courts for 25 years, her whole life—but he speaks almost no English. Of his three older siblings, one is in the second grade at nine, a seven-year-old has been diagnosed with a learning disability that nothing is being done about, and a six-year-old is in the first grade, just where she should be, doing well. "This is not uncommon here, one out of four," Mercedes Espinosa told me as if she were commenting on someone else's family. She is far more comfortable speaking English than any of her children are. Unlike Alicia, as lean and hungry as Cassius and conceivably as dangerous to the authorities, Mercedes Espinosa is very fat, bulging everywhere. She fit no stereotype, however. She was as far from jolly, as far from being content, as Alicia.

"One out of four gets along in the Courts," Mercedes Espinosa repeated, referring to Alazan Apache. "The others will all have many children of their own, and they'll start early like I did. I wanted my first baby so much. After that, the others just came. Too many too soon. What chance do they have from day one? What chance do I have? I blame myself really, but I wish I had a half-nice neighborhood for them to grow up in. From day one, you know." Mercedes Espinosa was somewhat plowed under by her situation, I thought, four children under the age of 10 and a husband present but not working. Her sister told me the husband drinks and sometimes beats her, an unrare combination among the people I was meeting. I wondered whether Mrs. Espinosa taking blame on herself was related to four early children, an abusive husband, being overweight, or all three. She was clear-eyed, though, about her environment.

Mrs. Espinosa pointed to a charred second-story apartment in Alazan Apache a few dull doors from her own. The windows were broken and the outside walls had been scorched. No one had yet boarded the windows, which looked like empty eye sockets. "Sprayheads," Mrs. Espinosa said. "Ten and 11 years old. They broke into the vacant apartment yesterday morning and put in a stolen TV set and VCR. After they had a party they torched the place. Six guys and two girls were arrested. They were all home by last night." Even the criminal justice system had washed its hands of them.

For both the younger children and the vandalizing sprayheads of Alazan Apache, I saw no direction that looked like up. They live in a different country undiscovered in our anthems, not one nation indivisible but a sternly partitioned land of no opportunity for those on the wrong side of the partition. From day one, as Mercedes Espinosa put it. My visit to Alazan Apache felt like a loss of bearings because I was mostly charting the invisible and chalking it up to the inevitable. The people I was seeing were lost, and therefore, in their presence, so was I.

When I last looked at poverty in San Antonio, in the late '60s, one-seventh of its population were poor. The city is now twice as large, and almost a quarter of the people are poor. Seventy-three percent of the poor are Hispanic. Forty percent of Hispanic children in San Antonio are poor. Racial and ethnic backgrounds are obviously, self-evidently, blatantly involved here. Meeting this manifestation head-on, I can arrive at no conclusion other than that white people who have money are fundamentally not terribly concerned about brown and black people who do not. San Antonio is the ninth largest city in the country, with a population of 1.4 million, and it ranks 96th in income level. It has the highest poverty rate among Texas cities. Fewer than one-tenth of the San Antonio children eligible for Head Start programs are enrolled. Existing programs are filled, and there aren't enough Head Start centers for the 90 percent who are unenrolled. Those who could build and fund new centers are not doing it. The Inman Center, Avancé, and Our Casas, along with other struggling agencies, are able to reach only a small percentage of those who desperately need their efforts. How much of this desperation, I wondered, was widely known in the gentler, more graceful sections of San Antonio that I had admired as I entered the city? And how much do the gentle people care if they do know?

I was feeling like a foreign traveler in my own country. A writer's notes are often disordered jottings that have no more ultimate use than an inventor's early contraptions on the way to the innovation he hopes will work. But I made a scribble that I think bears repeating even at this distance, even at the peril of a guilty plea to naivete: "The nation I'm becoming acquainted with is so different from the one I think I know that I must be in some third world backwater."

I went north to Oakland, wanting to see what a city does when its power structure has changed colors. Across the bay from San Francisco, Oakland is often known among whites as the place to avoid on the way to Berkeley. Along Broadway, the city's old commercial spine, you see block after dispiriting block of vacant storefronts with "For Lease" signs in their windows. But looking further, you see it's not so simple. In a number of ways the city has made a successful transition from being the fiefdom of a few old white families to becoming one of the first American cities largely run by black officials and businesspeople.

A degree of cultural integration is displayed in Oakland that is still rare in the cities controlled by traditional white establishments. There are working-class and middle-class neighborhoods where blacks, whites, Hispanics, and Orientals live side by side in what a local white reporter described to me as "friendly and unselfconscious diversity." Though the downtown section is almost lost to its former retail merchandising, new service industries thrive there, particularly in government and transportation. Thousands of employees come downtown every weekday, which is good for stationery stores and restaurants if not yet for department stores. A federal building opened in 1993 in the heart of the city, and the waterfront has one of the richest ports in the country.

Where does this leave those at the bottom and their children? It leaves them in place. The older and blacker the city, the more rooted its underclass, the easier it is for childhood to become a minefield.

The morning I arrived in Oakland I watched a group of boys and girls, none of them over eight, happily playing kickball and jumprope on their school playground. I was in West Oakland, barely a mile from downtown, where this neighborhood is referred to variously as "a wasteland," "a dumping ground," "no place to invest," and "exhausted." For the moment none of those words seemed to apply. Vitality and even joy piped out of the playground like show tunes. I stood outside the playground's cyclone fence next to another man who also watched the children, looking wistfully at their games. I exchanged a smile with the stranger, both of us recollecting our lost childhoods. He was the first citizen of Oakland I met. His name is Jeremy Holland, and he is a murderer.

Jeremy Holland knew none of the kids in the playground. He was simply spending a few minutes away from his troubles, and the troubles he causes, watching children play. When we introduced ourselves he was polite and talkative. "Keep small fry like that from becoming the grownup you're looking at," he told me, as though I were in charge and he were pointing out some third party that lurked in the stagnant municipal landscape waiting to pounce on innocents. More about him later, with the adult underclass. For now, among the Oakland schoolchildren, meeting Jeremy Holland helped me see that while no urban neighborhood is free of crime, the Oakland ghetto undoubtedly provides one of the higher ratios of outlaws per student.

Proportionately, Oakland may also have more agencies directed toward combating inner-city poverty than any other American community. One organization I was particularly impressed with is Jubilee West; among its activities is an after-school program that seeks out problem children. The most visible counselor was a math teacher named Charles Johnson, a tightly muscled, large man who looks and moves like a professional athlete. Johnson, known always as CJ, oversees the afternoon classes and takes the children on field trips, often to museums and libraries. He tries to make the afternoons fun for the students, and at the same time he tries to be candid with them about their environment.

CJ told me about one of his field trips with the Jubilee children, an outing that revealed their orientation and an ominous future. "I decided to haul them down to juvenile court," he told me. "The idea was for this to be an object lesson. I guess it took. 'I don't *ever* want to be in here again!' they said. The most frightening sound was the door closing on the holding cells in back. When the kids heard that, they all shuddered. But they had a question: 'Why is it just *us* here, everybody black?' That one I couldn't answer, but I told them it's worth remembering that California now has a majority of minorities."

Hearing this from CJ—"Why is it just *us* here, everybody black?"—I saw the gulf opening up between these children and my own, my 13-year-old who already has her route mapped to a world-class legal practice, my 14-year-old who breezily assumes he will design the structures your children are going to live in. I also began to understand Toni Morrison better, why her novels are read one way by blacks, a completely different way by whites. When their environments are pervaded by racism, black children and white children may live in the same town but not in the same universe.

There is never a moment in the lives of these children at Jubilee West when they feel on the same footing with children in the white nation. They may have helpful role models, but "equal" is not a word they grow up feeling comfortable with, as my children do. CJ will save some of them from carrying on losing traditions, that much didn't seem an unrealistic expectation to me. It was obviously beneficial to have a strong black man helping run a program that serves children living in a ghetto where fathers are scarce. But "equal" is like a distant object you have to squint at. I tried to see through CJ's eyes. "Would you say," I asked, "that race determines a child's future as clearly as it does his pigmentation?" "Let me count the ways," he smiled. "Let me count the ways."

We were standing in a corridor outside several of the Jubilee classrooms when a scream silenced CJ. There was an eruption in a classroom I had visited earlier. CJ rushed into the room to break up an argument between two 12-year-old girls. The only firm Jubilee West rule is that children are not allowed to hit each other, and these girls were avoiding a physical fight only by supreme efforts at self-control. They were standing on opposite sides of the room hyperventilating with rage and shouting, fairly dying to get at one another's bodies with fists and nails. Repeating the Jubilee no-fighting rule to them, CJ calmed them down and got them back into their seats. "Doesn't matter what you were arguing about, young ladies," CJ said, "because it's now finished. Back to work. When class is over, you'll shoot some baskets with me." Glands beginning to act up, CJ told me afterwards, overstimulating them all the time. He saw it first in the girls, maybe a year later in the boys.

Regardless of the homes these children came from, Jubilee seemed to be working to their benefit. Not only did it occupy the risky hours between school and darkness; the program also taught the children how to study and channel their impulses. But in the neighborhood it served, fewer than one child in 20 was enrolled. The supply was nowhere near the demand. If nature abhors vacuums, how does she feel about asymmetry? I was finding extreme poverty among children. I was finding people who wanted to do something about it. I was also finding—and feeling—frustration that so little is being done for so many. Where are the extra teachers for all the unreached students? In a city with too many vacant buildings, why can't more of them be used for after-school programs? Why isn't the proud new federal building funneling out counselors, teachers, catchers in the rye to help the children of West Oakland back from the poverty abyss? Was I expecting too much of government? What's government good for anyway? Where are the after-school programs to sweep far more of Oakland's children off the streets in the afternoons? CJ and his fellow teachers had a few brooms to try to deal with a sandstorm.

My next stop was Chicago, where the battle against extreme poverty has been going on longer and where the agencies that fight it are larger and more institutionalized than in Oakland. Public housing in Chicago was created specifically to give the poor a chance to leave the broken-down slums that fester in old cities. Programs that help children have won national attention for their versatile attack against the array of conditions that engulf the underclass.

Growing up on the South Side of Chicago, my father held the local YMCA record for the 100-yard dash, and it wasn't because anybody ever chased him home. These days a child doesn't even have to be outside his own housing project to be run breathless. If he or she refuses membership in a gang, or is coming home from a friend's apartment when crossfire begins, or simply looks the wrong way at a dealer, the child had better have a rabbity pair of legs. It's a safe bet my father's record is broken every day of the year in the neighborhood where he spent his childhood.

Two blocks from his old brownstone, though, three very small boys are starting out fairly lucky. The mother of three-year-old Louis, two-year-old Gabriel, and nine-month-old Marvin (after Marvin Gaye) has enrolled them in the Parent Child Center. The PCC houses a different program for each of the three boys. Louis is in Head Start, already learning to recognize the written labels—

"toothbrush," "picture," "doll," "cot," "Christmas tree," "red,"
"pear," and so on—that appear on many of the objects around the
cheerful room where he spends his mornings.

With large, dark, serious eyes that contrasted with the splashy
paint colors he had spilled on his smock, Louis wasn't at all shy
about talking to me, though he wasn't in an answering mood. "I ask
the questions," he said precociously, his smile showing that he
already had all his teeth. He rapid-fired his questions. "Why are you
here? Are you going to be our teacher? Do you know my mommy?
Didn't I see you on the TV? Naw, but you the *brother* of the
weatherman? Where you come from? Where you going? Why are
you here?" After Louis made the full circle with his questions, he
volunteered that he'd like to talk to me some more but he had to go
get his spaghetti now. Louis's mother, Dinah Lou Freeman, said her
son wouldn't have dared talk to a stranger, much less a white
stranger, much less ask questions, before he entered the PCC
program.

Louis's little brother Gabriel is in the toddler program, where he
listens to music while he learns to play, to share himself, with other
children. This learning to share is at the heart of the PCC. One of the
worst ghetto difficulties, particularly now that the middle class has
gone off to better neighborhoods, is for a child to gain the confidence
that will allow him or her to trust someone else enough to relax and
make a friend. Looking at Louis, Gabriel, and the other PCC
children, I thought of the way the poet William Blake viewed the
terrors and pleasures of childhood.

Blake saw each newborn baby as a point of perception at the
center of the circle of his or her environment. Everything that isn't
the child or the child's mother is outside the small point of
perception, strange and fearful. As he or she learns progressively that
parts of the environment are safe, the point of perception enlarges.
The world enlarges. At length, the grown child has expanded his or
her point to the degree that it is no longer a point but has become a
circumference. To William Blake, the goal for each person was to
become the largest possible circumference of perception. (Walt

Whitman put it another, similar way: "I am large, I contain multitudes.") On the South Side of Chicago, isolated children from the poorest families have points of perceptions that expand no farther than the door of their apartments and sometimes not that far. Nothing else is safe. Watching the PCC children take halting little steps toward one another, able to toddle trustingly for a few moments in the direction of someone else, I thought that the job of dilating points into circumferences probably has no equal in the raising of our young.

Marvin, Dinah Lou Freeman's nine-month-old baby, a corona of curls framing his round face, spends his time with the other infants, being held, learning to crawl, trying to stand up. The three Freeman children appeared well nourished and were described as being in excellent health by the PCC social worker. Parents who have infants or toddlers are required to be present in the PCC, so the boys' 24-year-old mother divides her time between the programs her two youngest sons are in and the parents' common room. The common room, containing only mothers whenever I was there, is a kind of social center. The mothers are encouraged to participate in outside activities that will lead to skills that could conceivably lead in turn to employment or at least a greater degree of self-reliance. The PCC's programs for parents (mothers, really) were far less developed than those for children. Even as a place to talk, however, the PCC common room was providing the mothers with a safe territory most of them would not otherwise have.

I had expected the Freeman boys' mother to be like several of her sorority sisters in the common room, staring vacantly, holding her breath until she could go outside to smoke, chatting idly about men or babies. Dinah Lou Freeman is, instead, their opposite. She has concrete plans for her sons and herself, and her hopes are intact. That doesn't mean they always will be, but when I found her in the common room she was studying a book on television repair, highlighting key passages, ignoring the kaffee klatsch around her. I watched her for a moment before interrupting her. Her wide eyes and the soft planes of her features give her a startled doe look. Her close-cropped Afro is, for the common room, uncharacteristically natural, and her bearing, even seated, is what would elsewhere be called regal. In any socioeconomic group but the one she was born into, her physical presence would have had Dinah Lou Freeman fending off modeling offers.

I was suspicious of myself here, having found an underclass woman with obvious ambition and the pleasing appearance that enable poor people, but especially poor minority women, to ascend the ladder from their backgrounds. Just the kind of person a white liberal can spot three soup kitchens away. Alfred Doolittle, Shaw's exemplar of the undeserving poor, would disapprove of Dinah Lou Freeman. This woman was too much like Doolittle's own daughter, the dreadful Eliza, clearly out to better herself. How could I generalize from her? I decided I wouldn't; I'd listen and learn.

"All three of my kids are doing so much better here than they would at home," Dinah Lou Freeman told me. "I knew I didn't want them sitting up in our project watching cartoons all day, and it's too scary there to take them out and about." Though her eldest son, Louis, is only three, she was already looking into magnet schools, which take the more highly motivated children and give them an accelerated curriculum that, school sponsors hope, will sustain and focus their learning abilities. "Right now my Louis is in the flow here, wondering about things and why they be the way they be," she said, stopping short at her colloquialism, smiling at herself. "I mean why they are the way they are. I want to keep that flow going for Louis." Like Eliza Doolittle, she was even correcting her language, easing it out of the ghetto; but unlike Eliza, she had no Professor Higgins.

Dinah Lou Freeman told me the story, the parable really, of the two tables. It is her version of how children get introduced to drugs in the projects. How they get lost and stay lost. "The neighborhood store is a few blocks away—dangerous blocks—so the gang will set up a little store of their own in an empty apartment," she said. "There are two tables, one for little kids, one for big kids. Nothing to sit down on, no chairs anywhere. They want to keep everything moving. The small children get candy bars and Coca Cola at their table, cheaper candies than they could get outside at the store in the neighborhood. Get some munchy crunchy for a quarter that costs 50 cents outside. Sometimes they'll get one free."

The empty apartment is run by a dealer. He gives the kids very good treatment, and they become loyal customers. Dinah Lou Freeman said the children start when they're five or six, attracted not only by the candy bars but by the independence of going upstairs to another apartment by themselves. "Then, when they're nine or 10, the dealer sends them over to the other table where he keeps the drugs. The brother who sits at that table, he's treating them nice, too, a little freebie of this, a little freebie of that. Sells them something for the weekend. Thimble of hash, snort of coke. Pretty soon it's all over."

Knowing the statistics on South Side children, having watched Louis and Gabriel and Marvin, I didn't ask the next question. I was wondering what the odds were that Dinah Lou Freeman could keep her sons away from the two tables. "I see what you're thinking," Dinah Lou Freeman accurately said without my asking her anything, "and I'll tell you this. These boys won't be going to those tables, no more than they can fly out my apartment. If I lose one of them to the tables, I lose him, but he'll know he's got a mama that's going to fight every inch every day." Dinah Lou Freeman is the kind of caring parent many of us don't quite believe exists in the underclass. I made a date to talk to her again about her own life and her prospects for improving it.

One hundred and twenty-five children are in the PCC, but the budget dictates that none can come more than three times a week. Most of the mothers are unemployed and receive AFDC, as Dinah Lou Freeman was. Only 30 of the 125 children have fathers recorded as being at home. The PCC coordinator, Franklin Jones, told me more fathers are around but they stay out of public view so the mothers can get welfare payments. He has counted five fathers who gamely show up for some PCC parent activities, though I saw none whenever I was there.

Franklin Jones himself is a ghetto success story. A studious man

who is a creative administrator (which I always think of as a contradiction in terms until I meet one of the rare ones), he grew up on the
South Side. His own father died young, and he was raised by his
mother. "The dads feel it's unmanly to be here," Franklin Jones said,
"in fact, unmanly to declare their fatherhood." He made a phone call
to another PCC center, remaking a schedule to accommodate a sick
teacher's absence, promising to move some surplus games into the
toddler program, arranging for a magician to entertain the Head
Start children. I was getting few glimpses of successful black men on
my journey, not surprising because I was looking at desperately poor
people. Still, it was refreshing to happen upon the PCC coordinator.
"Such a gift, to bring a child into the world," he said, "and the men of
this neighborhood do it as casually as they throw dice. Nothing
much to live for themselves, of course." Franklin Jones, having
grown up on the South Side as a fatherless black child, shook his
head sadly when he reflected that in his old neighborhood it was
thought unmanly to be a father.

Leaving the PCC, I remembered this was my father's old
neighborhood as well as Franklin Jones'. I began thinking about
fatherhood. My father was a father for well over half his life; I myself
have been a father for over half my life. Fatherhood is a state, a
relationship, I have occupied more comfortably than any other. I
know—with some chagrin—that I've behaved better and more
consistently as a father than I have as a husband or even as a friend.
Fatherhood is such a gift, as Franklin Jones said, yet here, on the streets
where my father grew up, it has almost no value. There are other ways
to raise children, of course, and Jones himself is a shining example of a
fatherless success, but for a father not to want to be a father was
probably harder for me to fathom than any other aspect of underclass
life. When I finished concentrating on children, I decided I would try
very hard to find the underclass fathers who don't care about their
offspring. Or at least who don't pay attention to them.

In a dangerous neighborhood without the protection of a father, a
child turns to whomever and whatever he can find—a gang, for
example—to provide some security. This is where the intervention

of an agency such as the PCC is most crucial at an early age, an intervention that is also a form of substitution. Among the successful parental supplements and substitutes in the Chicago ghetto, the most widely known is the Beethoven Project in the Robert Taylor Homes on the South Side. Fifty percent of the mothers with children in the project are teenagers. All are black. No one there would even try to estimate the percentage of drug involvement. The Beethoven Project's primary goal is to provide intensive help for poor families, from prenatal care for mothers through developmental education that prepares the children for school.

The nature of the community is displayed in what you have to do to get inside the Beethoven Project. In terms of security, the Robert Taylor Homes building that houses the project is a cross between a penitentiary and a top-secret government installation. If there were such a thing as a high-rise dungeon, this would be it. The outside door to the building is double-locked. Inside, two security guards check identities. A second locked door protects the stairway leading to the second floor, where the Beethoven Project is located. A third lock protects the headquarters of the project itself, and a fourth lock was on the door of the project official who had locked it merely to walk the few paces to the reception area to greet me. Thick wire mesh covers every window in the project.

The project official, when she had finished unlocking and relocking everything necessary to get me inside, was gracious, but she never stopped being cautious. "Everything here that's not locked can walk, and does," Haroldine Bourelly said in explanation of her extreme wariness. She is a doctor's widow who works at the project and is somehow able to be both upscale and down-home at the same time. Detailing the classes, activities, and programs with which the project helps children and their families, Mrs. Bourelly summarized its educational aims for me. She sighed when she reached the familiar part about the project's biggest obstacle. "We knew about drugs when we came in, of course, but we never dreamed their presence in the households was so major, so pervasive, how much they affect even the families that function best."

In my travels through the underclass, the role of drugs in their lives kept coming up. Drugs are classless, that's a given in contemporary society. Among the middle and upper classes, drugs destroy health, marriages, careers, families. Among the underclass, with the exception of careers that most of the chronically poor don't have, drugs do these things, too. But they also do something else: They block the exits. For the underclass, drugs are like padlocks on all the doors that might lead to somewhere else. Paradoxically, they are the escape that makes escape impossible.

The goal of the Beethoven Project is to open the underclass exits for young children. Mrs. Bourelly said the project, which has a national reputation, is frequently praised for getting youngsters up and running, occasionally blamed for not living up to expectations that it would revolutionize childhood on the South Side. It seemed to me a singular effort, comparable to having a garden club in the crater of an active volcano. I did not find an easy irony in the project being named for the composer of *The Pastoral Symphony* and *Eroica*. The project is far from pastoral; it is always heroic. Period. The young lives it saves would be lost to neglect even before drugs if there were no Beethoven Project.

Mrs. Bourelly listed a number of neighborhood triumphs, South Siders who went on to successful careers. The trouble was, in all the triumphs, the cases of successful escape, escape is the operative word. The neighborhood exists now in a state of abandonment. Most of the black middle class has managed to light out for greener pastures, and the white urbanites wouldn't be caught dead—or fear they would be—in this part of the South Side, which is a few broken, tumble-down blocks and a galaxy away from the University of Chicago. The neighborhood is left to moulder, recycling its own deprivation. When I mentioned the social isolation to Mrs. Bourelly, she nodded. "Some of the ones who made it do come back—there are pro basketball players who conduct clinics and so forth—but I'd like to see a lot more in a variety of different fields, not always sports or entertainment."

She herself does remain on the old turf. Black though light-skinned, widowed though ardently alert to the future, upper-middle-class though devoted to the children of the ghetto, Haroldine Bourelly is an exception to the rule that prosperous escapees don't look back. "You take one step at a time," Mrs. Bourelly said modestly. "You aren't going to make more than a little dent each day. But you want to keep making those dents until they add up to a wedge that a child can squeeze through. I've had such a good life, and now I want to give something back, and this is what I can do. So I do it."

When the early childhood programs are over, children go on to regular public school. Far from the Beethoven Project but in an equally stricken Chicago neighborhood on the Near North Side, I visited the Jenner Elementary School. Remember playgrounds—where you let off steam, learned to play and defend yourself, chose up sides, endured the early wins and losses that helped make you who you are? Forget playgrounds at the Jenner School.

This is the neighborhood of the Cabrini-Green housing projects, where the director of the local medical center told me 40 percent of the babies are born with cocaine involvement. Consisting of both high- and low-rise buildings, Cabrini-Green was once considered a model of contemporary public housing. That was two generations ago. By the '90s almost three-quarters of its residents were receiving some form of public assistance, and the area looks like a neighborhood abandoned after a war. This is deceptive because the war is still going on. At the Jenner School, where the students and teachers I saw are all black, no one goes outdoors for recess. The school has what is called a "closed campus," which means once you're in the building you can't leave. If a child would go outside for recess or home for lunch, he or she might not make it back. Gang battles are waged at all hours, turning the community's open spaces into combat zones. Shots have been known to rake the playground in the morning when the children come to school, at lunchtime, and at 2:30 when classes end. To make sure the students live through the schoolday, the principal cannot allow them to play on the playground.

Sharon Hicks-Bartlett, one of my guides at the Jenner School, is a young sociologist from the University of Chicago. She once lived in

Cabrini-Green and went to the Jenner School. "The worst thing that used to happen to me," she recalled, "is that kids were always stealing my lunch money. There were gangs then, too, but the fights in those years were only at night, and they only affected members of one gang or another." A teacher's aide at Jenner told me about a seven-year-old shouting at her in the former playground, which is now a parking lot, "Hit the ground, Ma'am! It's starting up again!" *Not allowed to use their own school playground!* Is this Belfast? Beirut? Sarajevo? Both teachers and students are told to enter and leave by the back of the school because the front is a battlefield. "These kids are amazing," the teacher's aide said. "They become experts at ducking and getting away." If you're old-fashioned enough to be stuck in the belief that schoolchildren are supposed to be learning different sorts of expertise, come to the Jenner School in Chicago.

A cartoon in the *Chicago Tribune:* The kindly, smiling teacher bends down to give what are evidently normal instructions to two very small boys who are on their way out of her classroom. The teacher and one of the small boys carry assault rifles. The other boy is armed with only a pistol. "Tommy has to go to the boys' room," the teacher says, "so, Jimmy, could you please lay down some covering fire while I secure the perimeter?" From the standpoint of pictorial precision, the only thing wrong is that all three people in the cartoon are white. Perhaps that was the cartoonist's concession to a political correctness that requires denial of ethnic reality on the *Tribune*'s home ground.

When I saw this cartoon, I realized that the warning from the seven-year-old at the Jenner School to her teacher, "Hit the ground, Ma'am! It's starting up again!" is as good a cartoon caption as the one in the *Tribune*. The humor, of course, is in the incongruity of the routine: gunfire in and around schools. A bleak irony locates itself in the survivorship of the very young. News stories from Bosnia are filled with this sort of pluck. The children of Chicago may be as uncannily adept at surviving as their counterparts in Sarajevo, but the two unavoidable facts are that they are in a society that regards itself at peace, and that they are prisoners in their own school.

In the Jenner School, which was an island of calm when I saw it, the teachers valiantly try to give their students the boost into a mainstream culture that is unavailable in their homes except where they are taunted by it on television. But Jenner is understaffed, undersupplied, and, in the combat zone where it is located, under-protected. Observing this, I thought about my own life in New York City, and the lives of most of my friends there. Almost all of us wring our hands over the public school problem at the same time we are washing our hands clean of public schools themselves. I know what I'm talking about because I *am* what I'm talking about. For 24 years—between 1966, when my oldest son began nursery school, and 1990, when we moved away—I always had a child enrolled in a New York City school. In not one of those years was it a public school.

Beyond the desire of most parents for their children to get a good education, there may be a reason for my avoidance of public schools more potent than racism, elitism, or even the fear of violence. Laziness. This is not to discount the other reasons—the terrifying superstition that poverty may be an infectious disease keeps close company with racism—but laziness is a magic carpet that transports parents toward private schools. I recall sending in the tuition, attending recitals and important games, and knowing my choice defined the world for my children. They played with the children of a neurosurgeon, a stock broker, a corporate lawyer, a movie director, an art dealer, and an executive vice president in charge of R & D. In the world of the private school, you know who belongs where. The rules for behavior and what TV the kids will watch are clear.

There is none of the uneasiness about behavior you associate, however unfairly, with the child of a maintenance worker, a shipping clerk, a welfare recipient. Your private school relieves you of that uneasiness. You show up at meetings occasionally to complain that your kid needs more encouragement in social studies or why did they have to pick *The Ugly Duckling* again for the spring play or couldn't the head of the middle school make his affair with the remedial reading teacher a little less obvious, but essentially you can forget about it. My friends and I could easily call the roll in New York City: Collegiate, Trinity, Brearley, Fieldston, Columbia Grammar, Dalton, Chapin, Bank Street, St. Bernard's, Horace Mann, Nightingale, Spence, Buckley, Montessori, and so on. Parents choose the one that turns out three-piece suits or the one that emphasizes the arts or the one that is most politically correct or the one that boasts of well-roundedness. Then you can relax.

I never had to think about my children's education on a daily basis. Instead, I did my part to widen the gulf separating races, classes, ethnicities, nationalities. As a start, the people who flee city schools for the suburbs or the private academies might consider acknowledging what we are doing to the schools, and the children in them, we leave behind. If middle-class blacks desert the ghettos, surely middle-class whites desert the public school system. Can anyone doubt that if people who can afford private education had to pay attention to the public schools in big cities, the schools would be markedly better?

There is a difficult issue here that has to do with the quality of education. It doesn't, all in all, seem a wise decision *not* to put your children in better schools that are available to them. I can't say that if I had to do it over again I'd be delighted to send my four children to just any public school. What was lacking in their schooling, however, was any melding with their neighborhood. There were elaborate interschool programs involving play productions, for instance, but all the schools were equally private. If the interschool productions of *West Side Story* and *Our Town* had been between a private school and the neighborhood public school, I don't think civilization's ramparts would have toppled. (In the case of *West Side Story*, involving gang fights, the casting alone would have provided an intriguing multicultural moment.) If other extracurricular activities similarly mingled children from public and private schools, it's difficult to come up with a scenario in which everyone would not have benefited.

The day after I visited the Jenner School, driving around the South Side of Chicago by myself, I became nosy enough to stop the car and observe street corner life, crawl slowly up some blocks and speed briskly through others. A few times I parked and simply walked around a neighborhood. Then I would drive some more. People were hanging out, waiting, selling, buying, soliciting, dealing. An underground economy was in operation, some of it legal and entrepreneurial, the rest of it also entrepreneurial but in merchandise that looked either to have been stolen or was illegal. As if I were visiting a third world bazaar, I saw everything from computers to sneakers being hawked on sidewalks, while corners and alleys seemed reserved for the mood-changing chemicals.

I pulled over at an intersection, parked, and headed into a side street. No one seemed the least bit interested in me, so I kept going. In an alley between two liquor stores, one of them boarded up, I saw a half-dozen boys, all looking like 10-year-olds, possibly 11, all in porkpie hats, playing cards. A pregang gang perhaps. It was a schoolday, and several of them were smoking. No Beethoven Project, no PCC, had set them on their course. Or maybe I was wrong. Maybe these boys had once been in programs that failed to get them to the underclass exit. I asked if any of them had ever heard of the Head Start program. Four of them didn't look up. One of them glanced at me silently, and another said, "I heard of it, I was in it. Long time ago, man." I followed up. "What did you think of it?" "It was nice. Don't mean nothin' now." Then one of the other boys looked at me and asked, "Hey, Mister, whatchoo want?" But it wasn't really posed as a question; it was more an order to stay out of his space. Off his turf. The circumference of his perception. They were only 10 years old, 11 tops, but there were six of them. And who knew who else might be in the wings, or what they might be carrying? I decided not to try talking to the card players anymore and kept moving.

Most of the buildings I passed were brick, and enough bricks were missing to give the structures a pocked effect. Neglect, apparently, is just as effective as shelling, if slower. Because of my ignorance about this neighborhood it seemed like a good idea to be prudent, but there didn't appear to be anything to be scared of. Not much was moving. My interest at this point was in children, few of whom were around.

The smaller children who were visible clung to the hands of the adults (mostly women) they tried to keep up with. I walked back to my car along a different side street, where two girls were having what sounded like a boom box contest. With different pieces blaring from their loudspeakers, each of the girls, who couldn't have been more than 12, tried to chant as fast as the rapper of her choice. They couldn't hear me when I asked why they weren't in school, and neither was willing to lower her blaster's volume. I wasn't being threatened, only ignored.

On a street where the garbage was piled so high I couldn't see several of the doorways, three toddlers were playing among the legs of two junkies who had nodded out. Were they the fathers? I wondered who was watching these kids. Two wore little parkas, blue and dark blue, which fit well. The other had a torn corduroy jacket that was much too large. He tripped over the shoe of one of the junkies. He fell onto the man's knees, but the man didn't move. The toddler picked himself right up and went on playing. The junky never noticed the child, never opened his eyes. This is how these kids were growing up, already surrounded by the land of nod. Remembering the parable of the two tables that Dinah Lou Freeman had told me at the PCC, I thought that procedure seemed almost benign—at least there was an element of choice—compared to what these toddlers were experiencing. They looked to be between two and three years old. How long before someone amused himself by slipping them some crack? Or had they already been prenatally infected, like Sherry Lane's snowbabies?

I went back to my car and drove around some more, slowly cruising the streets, peering into vacant doorways, trying to read the vacant faces I saw. Watching the toddlers had made me see everything I looked at as if I had their eyes. This was their world, what they had to work with. I decided it stopped being scary as long as they weren't being hit, and the known world probably remained a very small place where there weren't a lot of changes or choices. Constricting but bearable. Then I decided I was soothing myself with this thought, that torture never stopped being torture, and it was only observers like me who stopped being shocked when we'd seen enough. Then I thought the toddlers, these little points of perception destined never to become circumferences, were possibly going to be rescued by drugs and not from them.

Driving through the toddlers' terrain, able to brake or accelerate on a whim, I felt like more of a voyeur than I had on foot. At length I was pulled over by two policemen in a squad car. Following their instructions to get out of my car, I said I wondered what my infraction was. They said they wondered what white guy could be so off his rocker as to prowl these streets. Apparently they'd been following me for some time, curious about my curiosity, speculating on my mission. I was thinking they must have their own trained way of relating to their beat, young white cops with olive complexions, southern European features, friendly smiles—friendly to me anyway. Probably they were both bringing up families who were nervous about where they went every day.

Answering their question about what I was doing there, I explained my research. "You're in the right place for underclass, all right," one of them said, "and you don't even have to look for it. But you won't need a book to tell your story. Three words will do it." I bit. "What three words?" The other policeman answered, "Dope, Dope, and more Dope." The first policeman described the way the violence happens. "One guy takes the other guy's bag to start it off, and he shoots it and gets happy. The other guy lifts the first guy's toaster a month later. Nothing happens for maybe three weeks. Then, three weeks after the toaster is lifted the first guy stabs the second guy. Takes time to develop, but every day on the South Side somebody's three weeks are up." "Watch out," the second cop said. "You're in a combat zone; civilian casualties are high." "Lot worse than 'Nam," the first cop said. "Places we saw you going we wouldn't go and we're armed." "Better get rolling," the second cop said, sending me back to my car before I could argue with them about whether drugs were a cause or an effect of being in the underclass, or whether they'd describe their own neighborhoods as drug-free.

I started thinking about Vietnam and then about Nicaragua

during the contra war, both of which I'd seen closely. According to the policeman, those battlegrounds would have been less threatening to my safety than this neighborhood. Though I am easily scared by virtually any physical threat and sometimes by things that pose no threat at all (like mice), I felt only a detached inquisitiveness at this point, unlike the sympathy I had felt at the Parent Child Center or the heart-in-mouth fright I later experienced in the West Side ghetto at night. I recall the little lecture to myself: This, then, is your third combat experience and when it is over you won't do this any more times because sooner or later if you keep acting like the dentist for lions and sticking your head in their mouths to see what the state of their teeth is, they are going to do what comes naturally to lions.

I took a plane from Chicago to Maine. I hoped I was discerning the patterns and problems of children in the underclass. What happened to them next? Did childhood in the underclass rule the next stage of their development entirely? What were the breakout possibilities for teenagers? But there was an attrition rate. The state of the underclass did not guarantee that I would meet my subjects at the next stage of their, and my, journey.

The week after I left Chicago a little girl wearing a green sweater and being pushed in her stroller through one of the projects by her big sister was shot in the mouth and killed by someone who was aiming at someone else.

4

Teenagers

Living in the Well

Things fall apart for teenagers. The center not only cannot hold; it often cannot be found. Puberty, menstruation, the disruption of childhood certainties; voices, complexions, urgencies all changing constantly. The call of the glands. Adolescence is especially difficult in our society, which has roped off the seven teenage years, labeled them impossible, and tried to interdict the supply of sex, drugs, rock and roll. Underclass adolescence has all this and less: few certainties in the first place, almost no money, frequently not much of a family to be supportive. Things fall apart for underclass teenagers, and they fall apart precipitously, catastrophically.

Continuing my journey to a new stage of life, I also went to a new place. Bangor, Maine, is an hour's drive from where I now live. It is almost completely white. It is a mix of country and town. Looking in my own backyard is easy, of course, but not looking there is an avoidance of the obvious. I would also be avoiding, in the context of my research, a concentrated area of white poverty.

Like other towns its size though less conspicuously than big cities, Bangor has its poor neighborhoods. One of them surrounds the brick building that houses the Salvation Army's soup kitchen, where free lunches are provided six days a week. Pens for the poor in American communities are bounded by street and avenue names no one knows better than real estate agents. The rest of us simply know not to go there unless we're looking for trouble. The pens are not only geographical; they are also economic, educational, and psychological. These can blockade underclass adolescence from productive maturity more effectively than a slum, but it is the slum that is most easily identified, the slum that becomes the pen for the poor.

Pens help us not see the very poor, of course, not to be reminded of them, just as the majestic walls and hedges surrounding the estates of the very rich keep us shut off from their luxuries. At both ends of the economic spectrum, the extremes of American society lived invisibly for a long time. Those of us in the middle did not have to be bothered continually by the unattainable opulence of the one or the unappetizing misery of the other. The rich still have their walls, but in the past decade some of the persistently poor have escaped their pens in desperation as, in the previous decade, mood-stabilizing drugs enabled so many mental patients to escape theirs. The very poor have blended with the former hospital residents to make the underclass more visible in the '90s, as well as larger, than it has ever been.

For a person in the underclass, the fact of his or her presence there becomes a virtual prison. When you are around people who feel so incarcerated, you want to know why, but you may also want to get away from the prison cell. In the Salvation Army's soup kitchen one day in Bangor, the realization slowly sank into me that I was as split as a Maine log before you throw it on the fire—dying to get out of there, dying to know more about my luncheon companions. Wondering about my reasons for wanting to abandon my journey right in that soup kitchen, so close to home, I understood my own need to have the very poor in pens where I didn't have to be confronted by them, by their discomfort that can so easily make my comfort uncomfortable. I can't say I stayed in the soup kitchen because sympathy overcame my desire to leave, or that curiosity finally defeated the urge to bolt, or for any noble reason that might have to do with helping poor people. It was more that I suddenly identified with a different sort of traveler on a different sort of journey. I stayed in that soup kitchen the way a mountain climber hikes ahead when he has set his sights on a peak too high and distant for his abilities, assailed by blisters, cold, shortness of breath, doubts that he'll ever reach the summit. He is more afraid of what he'll think of himself if he turns back than if he keeps going. That's the only reason.

Though it contains just 33,000 people, Bangor has elements of a city. An international airport, a chain of Mr. Paperbacks, a Marriott, a squabble of lawyers, a symphony orchestra whose late conductor had the appropriately Middle European name of Torkanowsky, a bagel store, ballet classes, year-round legitimate theater, a large university nearby. It is the only place of any municipal size in its part of the state. But Bangor also has aspects of a frontier town— Victorian mansions built by the timber barons, a gigantic statue of Paul Bunyan and a lot of men who wander into town on Saturday nights looking like him, women whose hands are worked raw by the time they're 30, a rough-and-ready quality to chance encounters that can become physical if the wrong (or right) word is uttered.

Some people call Bangor the Hobo Capital of the world though it can't be if only because it's not as centrally located as, say, Wichita. The poor come to the Bangor soup kitchen from all over the chronically depressed rural counties of eastern and northern Maine. To go among the poor in Maine is to be reminded that persistent poverty is not exclusively an urban condition any more than it is confined to black and Hispanic people who are corralled into our large cities.

At the Salvation Army soup kitchen I met an appealing straw-blond teenager—tense, smiling, distracted—who looked as though he had seen extended jungle combat and had at last been given leave to make his way not to Bangor but Bangkok. Kelso Dana, Jr., 19 years old, was sometimes called Psycho by his friends. He wore a checked lumberjack shirt, a pair of torn corduroys, and a blue jean jacket with rock band decals on it. His companions focused on him, tousled his hair, asked him how he felt, told him what they did last night. He surprised me with a question as I watched him finish his Jello dessert. "Where you heading?" he asked me, though we had not yet exchanged a world.

At that point, not wanting to intimidate any of the teenagers, I said only that I was interested in kids who ate at the soup kitchen, where they came from, what they did. "Ho, that's a long story for a short page," he said, looking at the small notebook I was carrying. He went back to his Jello and his attentive buddies. I decided to give them their space, but I also wanted to keep track of Kelso, whose friends called him Kelso and Psycho interchangeably. His appeal to his contemporaries, as well as his openness with me, suggested that he could show me some of what I wanted to know about kids his age in a general state of dispossession.

Bangor is small enough that I did not have to wait long before running into Kelso again. Downtown after lunch, I saw him pocket some chapstick and a bag of M & M's in a drugstore. Instead of running out the way his friend did when the assistant manager saw him in the convex mirror, Kelso giggled nervously and handed the stolen goods back. The assistant manager let him go.

"Psycho, man, can't you be cool?" asked his friend, Bull Penner, when Kelso caught up with him down the block in front of a music store. Bull had gotten out of the drugstore with an extralong telephone cord, a Nerf ball, and a large jar of peanuts. He was starting to eat the peanuts, he was going to give the Nerf ball to his little brother, and when I asked him what the telephone cord was for, Bull said he'd give it to his girlfriend so she could stretch her phone all the way to her bed and talk to him before she went to sleep. I asked whether Bull had a place where he could call his girlfriend at night. "Naw, I'll go to a phone booth. She don't have no place either, but sometimes she stays over with her grandmother. She can take the cord around with her."

The night before, Kelso had gone to St. Joseph's Hospital in Bangor. "I slept there," he said. "They admitted me for overstress. Sometimes I just get so nervous." He grinned and put his head against the wall of the music store. Kelso has the open, cheerful features of the kind of athlete who used to be put on Wheaties boxes before Michael Jordan reinvented basketball. He had seldom done drugs, Kelso said. It was just that things got too much for him about once every three weeks. With his head lolling against the wall, Kelso—or Psycho—appeared as if he might still be a bit tranqued from whatever they gave him at St. Joseph's or whatever he was able to scarf up on his own. His friend Bull looked at a guitar in the music store window and seemed to be calculating his chances of lifting it.

Kelso and Bull entered the desert kingdom of losers, the psychological underclass, at leave five years earlier when they dropped out of junior high school. This concept of a psychological underclass presented itself to me when I saw the decisions made by kids younger than Kelso, just entering adolescence. No one has believed strongly in them, and they see no reason to believe very strongly in themselves. This absence of belief in themselves is their biggest problem. With wills gone to seed, egos in a coma, they have decided that they will fail at whatever they try to do, so why bother to do it? Adolescence is the exasperating interval when self-definition is achieved at the price of innocence; a child either makes the transition to the responsibility of adulthood or stays frozen in patterns that repeat and repeat his or her childhood in the effort to get it right once and for all. It's convenient and smug to say that direction is supposed to be provided by parents, but in the underclass a guidance system is not necessarily available. Parents can do worse than give no direction. They can, and in Kelso's case did, give the worst of all possible directions.

As he began to talk to me, Kelso became even more of a kid, a big, raw, Nordic kid with pleading hazel eyes, tangled hair, chiseled chin. He smiled so easily, seemed so ready to be helpful, that his tale, and his details, detonated against his extreme gentleness. But his appeal lay in his vulnerability, enhanced even by a disturbing bluish tint to his teeth, which were clearly in need of dental attention.

"I've been on my own since I left home up the County when I was 12," he began. Whenever anyone refers to "the County" in Maine, what is meant is Aroostock County, a vast rural shire that begins 100 miles north of Bangor and reaches to the Canadian border. It is distinguished by potato farms, forests, and sparse population. "There were six of us kids in all, and the others were older, off in the army and stuff. One of my big brothers would come home sometimes and play with me. We'd climb trees or pretend this old well out back was a basketball hoop and shoot rocks into it for points. Mostly, it was just me at home though. My mother would split on us, and then I'd be alone with my dad. My father has a drinking problem and was violent; he tried to slice my throat with a beer bottle and he'd whip me."

To show me what he meant, Kelso displayed whip welts on his shoulder and a scar on his neck. The social worker who knows Kelso best, and has known his family for years, confirmed the essence of his story and many of the details I found so hard to believe and impossible to forget. "My mother came back one night when I was 10," Kelso continued quite eagerly as he and Bull and I walked away from downtown toward a park in Bangor, "and she and my father disappeared into their room. The next morning we had this nice breakfast, French toast and sausage. Everything was fine."

Kelso stopped, and his face became blank. He had been so keen to tell about himself only a moment before; now he seemed disengaged, his eyes fixed on something in the distance. I thought he had possibly lost interest in what he was saying. Perhaps this was simply a boring interlude of family normalcy in his abused childhood.

"Psycho, man, you don't have to go into it," Bull said to Kelso.

"No, of course not," I hurried to agree, bewildered.

"So afterwards," Kelso went on, paying no attention to either Bull or me, "when breakfast was over, this huge breakfast my mom made, she walked out the front door, I thought maybe to pick a flower or go see if there was anything in the mailbox. My father took me out the back door, tied me up with a rope, and put me down in his well, this well me and my brother used to throw stones into. He left me there, my father did. Nine days. Maggots and leeches down there. I shouted but nobody heard me or if they heard me they didn't care. It was like the streets in a way, the streets I knew later, but I didn't know the streets then. I was living my life down there in that well, and I was on my own. There was a frog I ate parts of; I found a few maggots but then I'd throw up. I would hear my father walk by the top of the well and laugh or swear every few hours."

Kelso was no longer gazing in the distance; he was looking straight at me, into his story and, I supposed, also plunged back into the well. "The first two days I was scared and panicky," Kelso continued, "but I wondered when he'd let me out. After the fifth day I figured he never would. I kept going, much less than me."

I was looking at Kelso very hard, finding it difficult to listen, almost ashamed for being hurt by this story because here is a boy who really is hurt. He *is* a hurt. Why were his teeth blue? I thought: Kelso is a *Jr.*, his father wanted so much to pass something along in his own image, didn't he? Now why can't we go up to Aroostock County and find this father, Mr. Kelso Dana, Sr., right now and determine the slowest, most painful method of torturing him and making him live all damaged as he has done to his son and name-sake? If Kelso is much less than himself, as he says, why should his father be allowed to be anything more? This teenager and his story— his reality—made me understand for the first time how horrific life can become for the underclass kid who has no relatives, teachers, or community, no governing influence he can depend on, nowhere to turn except to someone who will hit him again and again. I asked Kelso where his mother was during the time he was in the well.

"Getting stoned. When my father finally pulled me up out of the well after nine days, I had a very high fever and it turned out I was almost dead from exposure. Before I passed out I saw my mom in a rocking chair completely out of it. He took me to the hospital. Told the medics I was lost in the woods overnight. Threatened to kill me if I said anything. I also got stab wounds from my father, and burn scars." He lifted up his checked lumberjack shirt to show smooth skin pitted in places where it looked as though he may have been napalmed. I was struck for an instant by the notion that there might be a disease that would cause this shredded effect. I thought of illustrations in medical textbooks. "Here, and here, and over here.

See." There were marks from lacerations where Kelso pointed, a number of other marks where he did not bother to point. The disease was Kelso Dana Sr.

Kelso tells this, and other details such as getting gonorrhea from an uncle, so that you cannot fail to see each picture as he draws it. He does not relate his tale bitterly, wrathfully, or even very sadly. He does not use his entitlements. *You* use them as you hear him speak. He merely supplies the facts; you supply the horror. In that sense he's a perfect storyteller. He does speak with feeling and spirit, with occasional jumps of anger, but mostly he keeps an even tone. He has been a reporter attending his own protracted torment, which in other people goes by the name of childhood. What if Lisa Steinberg, the New York girl whose father tortured her to death, had lived? Would she have grown up to be Kelso Dana? How much better would that have been? Kelso is a triumph of survival in a way, and in another way his problems are only beginning. At 19, he is a strapping youth, and I asked if he ever hit his father back.

"Ha ha. Whoa, you don't hit back when you're this high"—he put his hand parallel to the ground and lowered it to his waist— "and he's way up here"—he finished the gesture by raising his hand as far above his head as he could reach.

How long did Kelso stay at home?

"I took off when I was 12, ran away to Georgia, but many other places too. Florida, Texas, California, New York, Virginia, North Carolina, South Carolina, Alabama, Mexico." The names roll off Kelso's tongue like Stations of his own Cross. "I hitched out to Santa Cruz and San Francisco. Later I grabbed a freight from Boston back to Bangor. Now I'm looking for some kind of cleaning work, maybe sweeping up after people. I've been staying in a rooming house in one of the big old mansions the timber guys built, but lately I can't meet the rent. I saw my dad a week ago, and my mother. They've straightened up some, talk like some stuff is their fault, but they think I'm an asshole because I have no money and don't want to come home. 'Home,' you know." He smiled so all his bluish teeth showed.

"My father really wasn't so bad compared to his father. My grandfather was a copy of Hitler. Still is."

Kelso was finished. His gaze returned to a middle distance, like a surveyor appraising the land he had just measured with his transit. I was not sorry he was finished. I had passed the limit of my ability to listen to Kelso for now. I needed to absorb what he had been telling me. He had compared the well his father threw him into with the streets he later roamed, the streets where I found so much of the underclass. Wells are to bring water, streets to bring goods and services, but not for Kelso. For Kelso both were hostile environments, each a subversion of his adolescence, the years when middle-class kids are growing and challenging. Growth and challenge were ruthless ironies for Kelso. In his household he grew and challenged at the risk of his life. In his impossible youth, he made the transfer from well to street, and both were nightmares. He delivered me a metaphor, his well, which informed my own journey. They stood for one another, the well and the street, Kelso's prisons, and they bound his destiny to their brutalities. I hoped Kelso was not in as much pain as he was able to convey, and I knew that in his time he had been in far more.

I turned gratefully to Kelso's friend, Bull Penner. He was only 17. A thick brown beard made him look much older. He is a tough kid who gets into a lot of fights, especially when he drinks. Assuring me he wins most of them, he seemed no more to be boasting than if he were issuing a storm warning to small crafts. It was not a warm day, but Bull's black t-shirt was sleeveless. He loomed over me, and when he swung his bare shoulders, the one scarred, the other tattooed with a death's head, I felt he could have knocked over a street lamp or uprooted an oak if he wanted to.

Only a brave bartender would ask Bull Penner for an ID. It was easy to picture him picking a fight in a bar, causing pandemonium, emerging after throwing chairs and breaking bottles with only a small cut above one eye. When Bull told me he comes from Brockton, Massachusetts, I was reminded of another great Brockton brawler and said, "Oh yeah, Rocky Marciano." "Uh uh, Marvin Hagler," he said, dating me as surely as if I'd been a redwood and he'd been counting my rings. Though I met him in late October, Bull gave reasons for coming to Maine that might be listed by the middle and upper classes. The summer weather is fine, the countryside beautiful. He added another reason. "Plus, this is the only place in New England I haven't been in jail." They stopped putting him in juvenile detention when he was 15, he said, because he was so big and hit so hard no one believed he wasn't 18.

At 17 Bull has a furrowed brow above his beard and wears a tiny silver earring in one ear. He ran away from home when he was 11, already in trouble at school and even with the police. Bull's father had introduced him to liquor when he was nine, which was all right with Bull, but his father slugged him once too often when he was 11, and off he went. Bull ran to Bangor, where his grandparents live. They raised Bull, sort of. He lasted in school through the seventh grade. "Since then me and my buddy Kelso been hanging out. Right, Psycho?" Bull glanced at Kelso, who had his head down, looking worried. I wondered which day of his imprisonment in the well he might be reliving. After finishing the eighth grade Kelso fell through various social cracks—couldn't make it in the higher grades, not judged enough of a problem to either himself or others to be institutionalized.

I stayed with Kelso and Bull as they strolled away from downtown to a park that contains a huge statue of Paul Bunyan, a Bangor icon. "Nice afternoons we, like, hang out here," Kelso said, kindly accepting me as a novice to whom things needed to be explained. But he had been keeping his head down most of the time since he finished describing his father's cruelty. We were shortly joined by Kelso's girlfriend Polly whom I recognized as having eaten at the soup kitchen. She is large, clear-complexioned, bosomy, and she hugged Kelso as if that was what she was on earth to do. When Polly kissed Kelso on the forehead he put his head up and she kissed him again, and he brightened considerably. She wore a red t-shirt sporting the name of a garden nursery where she enjoys working, she said,

"Because plants can't hit back." She took Kelso's hand. At her touch, Kelso relaxed and smiled his most undistressed smile, at peace for a while.

Kelso, Polly, and Bull were joined in the park by other teenagers, all of whom seemed to be waiting for something to happen, something that might give them guidance or at least lend their day some shape. This is not so unlike teenagers who have far more advantages, but with these kids there was a dead-end quality to their activities. Hanging out with them as they hung out with each other, I saw the quality of vagabond randomness their lives had. The randomness existed not only in the lazy afternoon, as it might for any teenagers idling after school, but also extended over time. They all found it difficult to look ahead with anything approaching clarity about goals. Adolescence is, after all, a moment that leads either into functional adulthood or long-term dysfunctional vagrancy.

One of the boys, Steve Gammill, 17, was playing hooky that day from Bangor High, where he was in the 11th grade. He said he smokes too much to play sports. His sister, Joey, was with him, along with her boyfriend, Fred, all of them playing hooky. The teenagers wore clothing and jewelry that, to me, held pain and disaffection in them. Several ears and one nose were pierced, rather raggedly punctured, which I can't help regarding, however squarely of me and however widely practiced in all classes, as a form of self-mutilation. Their t-shirts carried inscriptions that schools are for suckers and that society doesn't work so why should we. Steve and Joey said their mother lives in Bangor, has no job, and receives welfare. They saw their mother twice last summer and not since then. Their father? "He's in Rhode Island or Texas, whatever," Joey said as if these two states were next to each other or as if, by naming the smallest and almost-biggest, she covered all the bases. "We might spend Christmas with my mother." Meanwhile, they were staying with a divorced aunt who lived in a trailer park.

Fred said he might become a cook. Joey, who admitted the last grade she'd actually finished was the ninth, said she thought she could be a secretary or a receptionist, sounding as though she might have seen a television show about a woman who had landed one of those positions. Steve was torn between which branch of service he would join. "Marines are lookin' for a few good men, but, you know, the navy gets the gravy." I had to press them to get any guesses at all about the future. The kids seemed to be waving in the breeze. "It could be cool to do nails," Joey said when I almost implored them all for some kind of vision of themselves in five or 10 years, "pretty ladies' nails, you know, or their hair, whatever. Until one of them would fix me up with her son." In this crowd on this afternoon, that statement constituted, however atavistic and antagonistic to ideals of gender equality, a real blueprint.

The general aimlessness here, it seemed to me, might have its source in two opposing, yet linked, views of their parents. In one sense, the parents had failed to provide positive models of admirable adults these kids might become, so they weren't bothering to become anyone. Conversely, the parents provided, simply by their presence, models as unencouraging as they were clear. The effect of either or both of these possibilities would be to persuade the kids not to grow up lest they become their parents. It would be a mistake to claim that white underclass youth have even less to look up to than their black counterparts, yet these particular Bangor kids were visionless in a way I found unique among all the teenagers I met.

In the black ghetto, the kids have unrealistic dreams, but they at least have deep wishes, things they can imagine themselves doing—singing and dancing like Paula Abdul, slam-dunking like Shaquille O'Neal. In contrast, these Bangor adolescents did not appear to have anyone they especially looked up to. When I asked whom they admire, I got only guffaws and a mocking reference to Phil Donahue. Not discounting the probability they were mocking me along with Donahue as members of the same out-of-it generation, it was still obvious these teenagers saw very little anywhere to respect or emulate. The statue of Paul Bunyan they stood beneath was its own form of mockery; the old lumberjack cuts a ludicrous figure, much less "hero," for these kids. None of them had read the stories about him, which highlighted their lack of connection to middle-class childhood.

Except for Kelso, who had compared his grandfather to Hitler, the teenagers all claimed to have grandparents who were or are respectable, not so badly off as they are. But this turned out not to be strictly accurate. I talked to social workers later who know these kids and their backgrounds. The majority come from generations of part-time workers, wanderers, families that never quite hang together. Joey and Steve Gammill, whose mother is on welfare, do not have a grandfather, for instance, who has ever had steady employment. It may be these teenagers have recollections that involve brutal or neglectful parents, recollections that rule out nostalgia for their own early childhoods. They must feed the hunger we all share for having had better times somewhere, so they locate the better times in the era of their grandparents—safely before they themselves were born. It is as if they were saying, Well, we used to be better off, but not in my lifetime. Only Kelso was unable to point to a redeeming past, and Kelso has lived with demons farther back than he can remember.

My request for future plans proved such a conversation stopper that the kids might have wandered away, or someone might have had the courage to tell me to get lost, if new blood had not suddenly been injected into the group. This new blood, it turned out, did have the courage to challenge me, and more. The newcomer was a boy familiar to all the kids, a dealer, whom they greeted both as Dr. Feelgood and Butterfly. His arrival was characterized by a sort of barging into the middle of the others, clearing a path for himself even though there was no crowd that might require any shoving. He looked 15 to me, 16 perhaps, and was stocky, almost squat.

Rippling with toughness, Dr. Feelgood confronted me imme-diately. "Hey! Don't put my name in the paper or I'll take your head off. What the fuck are you doing?" He walked away but didn't leave; he circled Paul Bunyan. When he calmed down, Butterfly-Feelgood talked about his own relationship to formal education as if he were a disgruntled shopper who has looked at several kinds of sweaters, melons, or couches, finding them all unimpressive. "I like finished the seventh grade, you know, and then after that I've tried other grades —a *lot* of other grades at one time and another, but I didn't care for them either, so I like shredded the school scene."

Two more boys wandered by. One had a black eye and introduced himself rather officially as Dick Brown, as though he were a well known public figure I should have heard of. "I do occasional work for the government," he announced. The other boy, Jimmy Lister, was only 15 but looked a worn and tired 30. I asked if he went to school today and what grade he was in. "Naah. I'm in the eighth grade, just didn't feel like going today." Where did he sleep? He gave a flick of his head so the earring hanging from one of his ears swung out a little. "Streets. I was gonna go to North Carolina or Florida for the winter. My father said he'd call the cops on me. It's cold enough now so I'm over at the Bangor shelter." Why not at home? "Home? Yeah, I forgot. I had trouble there. Couldn't take any more shit, my father batting me around."

Dr. Feelgood wanted to be the center of attention again. "That's the kid I knocked the fuck out of the other day," he told me, pointing to Dick Brown. Then he turned to his recent victim. "But hey, now we're friends, right, you fuck?"

Dick Brown nodded. He gets beaten up a lot. It turned out he did work for the government in a way because he's known as a dealer squealer. He is not exactly free of substance abuse himself. Kelso's girlfriend Polly told me Dick Brown went into convulsions recently and then into an alcoholic stupor outside the Bangor shelter. Kelso said that Butterfly kicked Dick Brown in the chest after knocking him down but did not give him his black eye. Someone else did that. "The guy's pretty well asking for it, getting people busted, isn't he?" Kelso asked the question so it contained its own answer.

Dick Brown and Jimmy Lister wandered off as they had arrived, in no particular direction.

The kids began to cut up, to be kids, to put me on, put each other on. They might have been performing for Dr. Feelgood, trying to impress him with their own swagger. "This dude says he's writing some book but, like, he might be undercover." "If you're cool, Dude, you'll score us a six-pack anyway." "So this, like, asshole cop comes up to me last night, Butterfly, and I tell him I'm totally clean and he's like, we'll see about that, and I'm like, where's your warrant, and that, like, chills him out." I made no move to leave, and the longer I was around them the more comfortable I became and the less they seemed to mind my presence. A peppering of quick answers came when I asked how often people in this group take drugs.

"Me? Drugs? Never," said Kelso, but everyone else snickered, so he added, "Not anymore." "Me, only weekends." "You wouldn't believe this, but I get 'em from my little sister." "Just the occasional joint, uppers if I can find 'em." "Like what else is there to do, man?" "When the drugs start, I'm outa here. Never!" "Black beauties when they're around." "You do what you do, no biggie, gimme a break, man." That was Butterfly.

To change the subject, which had gone as far as they were going to let it, I asked Christine Masella, a pretty 16-year-old brunette with a stye in one eye, if she could name a dream she has for herself. I still wasn't satisfied that there weren't more focused ambitions here. Christine's appearance, I thought, held some promise of a future. With her hair done up neatly in a red ribbon and her neck arched expectantly, Christine might have been on her way to something. She said she would finish school and go to work, but I wanted to know more. Beyond the general goal of a job, did she see herself in a particular place or in a particular line of work? My timing was poor; the kids were already smelling the evening.

"Haw," said Charlie Hegan, a cocky 15-year-old wearing a blue-and-white bandana around his head, "Christine's dream is three guys at one time."

Everyone laughed and said that was true. No one laughed louder than Christine herself. "My dream," she said cheerfully if somewhat hesitantly, "is to be a senator—or a photographer." More laughter, this time in derision.

"Christine likes to bang," Butterfly the dealer offered helpfully, "but she don't mean nothing by it."

All the others agreed, chorusing after Butterfly, that they didn't mean anything either.

These were not the "troubled teens" of suburbia. As I left them I was thinking their connection to the American mainstream was as tenuous as if Paul Bunyan, logging days over, had dreamt them into existence to amuse his blue ox. Suburban teenagers may have lost their anchorage. These Bangor kids had no anchorage to lose, no mooring to slip away from. They were in a whirlpool that merely carried them around in a circle. Without a past that nurtured them, without a past they can even tell the truth about, it can be no surprise they also lack the capability to envision realistic futures. It is not merely that they resist growing up and prefer to daydream typical teen fantasies; they do not even have the programming to seriously consider adult life. I was curious about the kind of outlook I would find among their big-city contemporaries, teenagers from the areas containing what sociologists call the impacted underclass. Was the danger of the streets a stimulant or a depressant, or both? Where did they see themselves heading? What helped them, what hurt them?

One evening in Chicago, after a long day at the housing projects, I went to Chicago Stadium for a basketball game. I bought a scalper's ticket and climbed to a perch high above the action, which had already begun. As I entered and looked down at the glowing rectangle that focused itself into the basketball court, my first sight was of Michael Jordan in the air. He made the air visible, giving it shape, form, and color, and, as he became the air, it became him for those elongated milliseconds while he hung in it. At length, he consented to loose his missile into its certain trajectory. As the ball swished, the crowd, which knew Jordan's miracles well, laughed with delight because he had just shown them one they had never quite seen before. "Oooooh, hoo hoo hoo," said a voice next to me in the dark. "Michael take it to the pane, don't he?"

Meet 16-year-old Rozzy, for Roscoe Overton. Like me, he was alone. Unlike me, he knew the names and records of every player on both teams, including substitutes. With his easy smile and a rounded forehead that held a mother lode of basketball lore, he looked to be the perfect companion for this game. He was leering so lecherously at my hot dog that I furnished him with a couple of his own before we got down to business. In the half-minute it took Rozzy to eat them, I reflected on whether he said "pane" or "pain" and what Jordan means to ghetto kids. He means a lot, of course, to millions of fans who admire his abilities and grace when he plays, but with black teenagers he enjoys a special relationship that has to do with unlimited possibility. He is forever making the impossible happen.

In Rozzy's case, no basketball career looms even as an impossible dream; he stands about five eight and a half on tiptoe, and he confessed he didn't actually play the game. But when he saw Jordan doing anything, for a little while he could do anything, too. He did not in fact mean pain as a bodybuilder means it when he says, "No pain, no gain." He meant only that Jordan soared to the glass backboard above the basket. But Rozzy's term, combined with his reverence, also suggested that Jordan exceeded the boundaries, was not stopped by the windowpane on the outside of the house. I saw that it was Rozzy's way of putting a good face on things. When we watched Jordan hobble off the court in the third quarter, barely able to walk I thought, Rozzy told me he was not injured but only sitting down briefly. He was right; within two minutes Jordan was springing off the bench back into action. The next time Jordan scored, Rozzy explained that "Michael's leapability" was what took him beyond the pane where no one had ever soared before. The leapability made possible the miracle.

Exiting the overheated stadium together into a howl of wintry air, Rozzy and I met three friends who were waiting for him, two teenaged girls and another boy. After Rozzy did a brief play-by-play on Jordan's dazzle for his friends, they explained what Rozzy was doing inside the stadium while they stayed outside. The four of them had sold a radio (where they got it I didn't ask), and Rozzy had won a coin flip with the other boy to see who would buy the cheapest seat to the basketball game. No one questioned the understood "right" of the two boys to contend for the ticket and leave the girls out in the December cold. I was introduced to the other three: Mombasa was the boy, his girlfriend was Merry May, and Rozzy's girlfriend was Kenisha. Mombasa cut a large, menacing figure (a little like Bull Penner), very sure of himself and of his dominance over Merry May, who was unmistakably pregnant.

We began to talk about their lives as we walked toward the West Side project where they all live. Both girls said they were "owned" by their boyfriends, their "men," though none of them had yet celebrated a 17th birthday. Kenisha explained that if she weren't owned by Rozzy she would be "free meat" for anyone else in their gang, the Vice Lords. The Vice Lords respect Rozzy because he's one of them and very quick on his feet, "so they don't mess with his woman." It became clear girls are warned that if no single gang member owns them, they may be gang-raped by the rest of the gang. But Kenisha, who is 15, also felt romantically toward Rozzy. She said she has liked Rozzy for a long time and was glad to become his property because before they made this deal he had been too shy to come near her. "She be mine now," wiry, sweet-visaged Rozzy explained, "so she be nobody else'."

Mombasa cut in. "Now Merry May here is having my child, you dig, and she be totally under my protection; nothing can happen to her."

I considered the time of night and where we were but went ahead and asked the next question anyway. Does Mombasa intend to share responsibility for the baby who will soon be born?

"That's totally beside the point, man. The point is Merry May is under my protection, you dig, and nobody's gonna mess with her." The breath of each of us was visible in the cold, but Mombasa's puffed out as combatively as if he had been a steam engine.

"My mama's gonna look after my kid," Merry May said.

Will Merry May live with her baby?

"Depends. Me and Mombasa may get a place, and my mama may get a bigger place, whatever."

All right, this was about possession, not responsibility, so I'll stay with that. I partly thought the ownership policy was a quaint children's notion, something vaguely like a Scout's creed. I could also see it as a kind of survival mechanism. But I was appalled at a ghastl irony I saw in this new form of possession, a repudiation of every thing black Americans have done to free themselves, from Na Turner's Rebellion to the marches and speeches of Martin Luther King. What if another gang takes a Lords woman?

"They be payin' for what they gettin' if we catch 'em," Rozzy said.

"They be payin' big time," Mombasa said. He is a hulking teen with big cheekbones that look like weapons.

Are some women available to the Lords as "free meat"? I recalled that Sharon Hicks-Bartlett had used the same term as Kenisha when telling me about the general availability of certain women to gangs.

"Depends how they be acting," Kenisha said.

"Joby's sister Lurleen used to be," Merry May said, and the others nodded thoughtfully.

"Till she got sick," Rozzy said. "Joby couldn't do nothin' about it 'cause he wasn't a Lord. After she got sick nobody wanted her anyway. Before that, everybody takin' turns on Lurleen—four, five, eight a night."

Would these four teenagers call that gang rape? When I asked this, they proceeded to conduct an elaborate semantics discussion about whether it was rape only if what happened was against Lurleen's stated will or if there was an understanding she was common property. The girls did most of the talking. Despite her "free meat" terminology, Kenisha considered it rape. "It's her body and there's no way that's how anyone wants her body used." Merry May disagreed: It was Lurleen's own fault because a gang member known as Rope offered to "own" Lurleen. She had turned him down; therefore, what happened after that was fate, not rape. With a can-I-say-this? glance at Mombasa, Merry May added that Mombasa used to go with Lurleen a bit but never wanted to own her and she was sassy with him anyway. "The woman don't know the meaning of 'shut up,'" Mombasa said, scowling as if, in describing Lurleen, he was also warning Merry May. Rozzy, trying to put a better face on things the way he had at the basketball game, said Lurleen used to like sex a lot on her own. "Lords wasn't exactly *forcing* her to do

all be getting high together and then they be falling on
e taking it."

y ever there?

t me." A look from Kenisha, who apparently knew
e time."

a said it all goes back to Joby, Lurleen's brother, who
ord's leader in front of a storekeeper. The leader, furious
blicly humiliated, not only blackballed Joby from the
swore to make him pay some other way. Lurleen was the
. I asked how Joby had insulted the leader. Mombasa said
d the Lords leader to buy him and his girlfriend a pint of
Lords leader, possessor of an ID, could buy liquor for
a dispensation of favor (charging a sort of corkage fee), but
t like to be asked by just anyone, and Joby was just anyone.
er felt he was being used. Like that: end of Joby's chances as
; beginning of his sister Lurleen's career as a sexual slave,
ended only when she became too ill to perform anymore.
I asked what her sickness was, they said it began with a
red appendix and continued into a succession of what Merry
called "women's problems."

anted to know what they thought their futures were. In Bangor
had been snickering when I asked what the teenagers might
me. These Chicago teenagers weighed the question as if they had
e some thinking about this themselves. All four mentioned
ertainers and athletes they admired. Though none expected to
ch stardom, they all seemed to be in some way inspired by those
o had. Michael Jordan and Janet Jackson, for instance, actually
ightened the lives of these teenagers. Turning toward what he saw
s his real possibilities, Rozzy said he was going to get into a job-
raining program. He had completed the ninth grade and was not
currently attending school. The trouble was, I found out later, the
program he mentioned often leads only to bussing jobs in fast-food
joints, which constitute their own kind of dead end. Still, he would be
off the streets if the training was successful.

Of the four, only Merry May was still in school (ninth grade), and she was going to quit when the baby comes, though she said a bit vaguely that she hoped to return and study what she called home management. Her only firm plan beyond having her child was to stay with Mombasa. Mombasa had completed the seventh grade, and Kenisha, like Rozzy, had kept going through the ninth grade. Kenisha was currently working part-time for an undertaker. "Part-time is as much time as I want to spend with them stiffs. I'm hoping to get me a taxi, which they're taking women now, when I get my license."

Mombasa at first was reticent, but when the others had all put forward some kind of plan, he loosened somewhat. Having done what he called "a little" dealing, Mombasa said he wanted to quit that and maybe get in the air force so he could become an airline pilot. "One way or another," Rozzy ribbed him, "you gonna get high." "You got that right," Mombasa said, and he and Rozzy gave each other low fives. "No, but really," he went on, "if they don't take me as a pilot, I'm an awful good mechanic and I might could catch on the air force that way."

All four kids have had cocaine but only Merry May and Mombasa admit to being fairly regular users. In the way Mombasa dominated her, there was the faint suggestion of an idea that Merry May is not only "owned" by Mombasa; she may be on her way to hooking to support both their habits. Her pregnancy, in a short time, could result in a snowbaby like those born to Sherry Lane in Los Angeles. What was most startling to me was that despite the presence of antidrug programs and pitches as omnipresent in the ghetto as in suburbs, none of these kids made any connection whatever between their current drug use and a severely limited, if not destroyed, future. They all thought, as Rozzy put it, that they were "handling" drugs, not that drugs might be handling them. Here his characteristic optimism shaded off into denial. All four knew people who had died of AIDS, but they also believed AIDS warnings were overdone, part of the adult world's antisex, antidrug propaganda campaign. "You no homo and you don't share needles," Mombasa said, "you ain't gonna catch AIDS."

We were deep into the West Side slum by now, and I was losing my nerve. I began to sense dread in the lifeless and wrecked streets we were on. Dread in the sidewalk shadows first, then in my freezing, ungloved hands, then in the shivering rest of me. It was well past midnight, and a blinking sign above a closed car rental office put the temperature at six degrees Fahrenheit. I concluded that it was too cold and too late for anyone to be out who did not have some dark purpose. It began to matter to me what my companions thought of me. If we suddenly faced some kind of trouble, would they protect or attack me? Was I someone they had gotten to know and possibly like a little, or was I simply an indistinguishable version of Whitey? Accompanied by these two Lords and their ladies, I was probably safer than I'd be inside the Loop downtown, but I was suddenly terrified.

How much longer could I count on their good will? I reasoned that I have children both older and younger than these kids. I shouldn't be afraid of them; I should feel protective toward them. This thought gave me only a moment's consolation before I began wishing I were with my own children, and the wish was succeeded by the fear, however irrational, I might never see them again. At a street corner we were whipped by an icy wind, and everyone was staggered, Merry May hugging herself and her unborn baby. Mombasa didn't put his arm around her, but plunged his hands deep into his pockets. What else was in those pockets? I began to be colder inside than outside.

We were in a territory that belonged only to the knowledgeable and the armed, and I was neither. What if . . . ? Conversation had ceased. It was too cold, too windy, or they were through with me, or I was through with them. A lone taxi meandered up the block we were on, bumping along the unrepaired potholes. "Thank you, thanks a lot, good luck all of you guys," and I was huddled in the cab. Was Merry May giggling, Rozzy flipping me the bird? They did not return my wave.

So what? I could descend this way into afflicted precincts where these people's reality was like a nightmare anyone else I know might have, then awaken grateful he'd only been dreaming. The teenagers I'd been with were stuck there, while I was only on tour. I could grab a cab back to any reality I chose. But I was, at this point, a tourist without bearings, further from any answers to, for, and about the underclass than when I began my journey with my predilections and sympathies intact. I was as impressed with how hard it is to understand the true predicament of the underclass from the outside as with how hard it is for those locked inside to escape.

These Chicago teenagers, for instance, were both struggling and surrendering. They'd all left or were leaving school, one of them to give birth to a child who may or may not have a father on the scene, who may or may not come into the world with a cocaine habit. Only one of the four—Kenisha at the mortuary—had a current legitimate means of support. At the same time, three of them thought they could look forward to the air force, driving a cab, a job-training program. Yet at present, not one of them was really doing anything that led to anything. They revealed a larger issue that abided among the underclass youth I met, forced to fend for themselves though also arrested in their progress toward a citizenship useful to either themselves or their communities. There was, finally, a strange weariness about them. They were old before their time, but they weren't really growing up.

I headed west again. I wanted to see if I could find teenagers who were making an effort to form families of their own, regardless of the backgrounds they came from. A month later, in Los Angeles, I met many more adolescents, two of whom were in the vast gymnasium-basement shelter of the Hollywood United Methodist Church. An Irish kid from South Boston and a Valley girl trying to unfry her brain. At 19 and 16, Justin and Bryna Gallaher were married and homeless. An immediate impression they made on me was one of eagerness. Her hands fluttered impatiently, eager to be busy, and his eyes would open wide every few seconds, rising into his forehead in a kind of nervous tic of eagerness. Justin and Bryna were eager about everything, eager to stay together, eager to please a stranger, eager to build a future better than their pasts, eager to get out of this church shelter that was lined, wall to wall, with army cots.

Shelters are little third worlds unto themselves. As in ghettos, a primitive barter economy operates. Your shirt for my cigarettes; your paperback for my toothpaste. In ghettos the quality of possession is consoling to the dispossessed, who can be proud that a few things are theirs alone. As I'd recently seen, gang members sometimes even "own" women. Ownership does not mean security; in a large shelter the temporary residents need to guard even their shopping bags. The principal complaints I heard about shelters are that both men and women get ripped off while they sleep by those who are able to stay awake, that women are sometimes raped by other women, and that shelters can turn into marketplaces for drugs.

The manager of the United Methodist shelter was Joel Sooby, an unemployed casting director on his way to becoming an inner-city schoolteacher. He was young and strong, two of the principal requisites for running a shelter. Against what I took to be heavy odds, he and an assistant managed to keep order in the vast gymnasium while fielding questions and complaints from overnight guests. "Where can I find me some shoes?" "Joel, how am I gonna get rid of my crabs?" "Will my general relief check come to the temporary address I left, or will they still send it to my old lady's place where I don't live anymore?" "This guy in the next cot, Joel, he smells something fierce, can't you put me somewhere else?"

When the shelter's 157 cots were all assigned, the muscular Joel Sooby strode to the front of the gymnasium and called for attention. In an instant, clamor became silence. "Good evening, guests," he said loudly but respectfully. "Good news, there will be a movie tonight before lights out." A murmur of appreciation came from the assemblage, but now Joel Sooby continued in an imperative tone I recalled from a few hundred nights in an army barracks. Only the lyrics had changed; the music was the same. "After the movie, there will be *no* sexual activity. There will be no sexual activity, even with yourself. You men, just keep it in your pants. No visiting in the ladies' section. Lights out at 10. Wake-up call is 5:30 A.M. Fold your blankets *neatly* in the morning and get yourselves going. There will be *no* fighting in here at any time. Have a nice evening!" When he finished, the clamor started up again, as did the petitioners approaching Joel Sooby with their problems. Unless it was only a piece of soap someone wanted, he could solve virtually none of these problems, but he listened patiently. Those who came forward appeared to respect both his firmness and his forbearance. I felt he was giving the homeless a sense that, for tonight anyway, they belonged somewhere, and here was someone who would pay attention to them.

Justin and Bryna Gallaher sat together on a single cot, holding hands, during Joel Sooby's announcements. In a generous departure from usual shelter protocol, Sooby permitted them to sleep on adjacent cots in the men's section instead of putting Bryna in the women's section. This way, although they still couldn't touch each other, Justin could protect Bryna from anyone else who tried to touch her. Justin was wearing dungarees and a black undershirt, boots he called black dingos. He could fling his long red hair until it almost touched the Zodiac tattoos on his upper arms. Bryna, too, has beautiful hair, auburn and soft, above her nervous, pleading eyes. They had been staying four nights at the Hollywood shelter when I met them. She has essentially been homeless for three years, since she was 13; he has been on his own since he was 15, homeless for much of the past four years. Surrounded by scores of homeless men of all ages ready to bed down, Justin and Bryna told me how they got there and how they think they may get out.

"I lost a baby," she said, "because of all the speed and pot I was doing. It was good I lost it actually; I hated the father. I was jumping around from place to place after my parents kicked me out. I wouldn't have been any good as a mother. I might be better now, I don't know. Maybe with Justin . . . " As her voice trailed off, I was still aware of the eagerness that impressed me when I first spotted her, but now I also saw how insecure Bryna was. She wanted a lot of things but had no confidence that she could actually get them or that she deserved them.

"When me and her met," Justin said, "I was getting jobs truck drivin', livin' in whatever truck I had latched onto. Trucks, ladies, booze, that's what I was into." Three years older than Bryna, Justin seemed to me slightly more focused. There was no bragging here, merely a recital of his youth. "I have this son back in Boston, we may get him out here."

"I wanna raise his son and have a family together with him, too." Bryna blurted this out as though she had to say it quickly, more to convince herself than to inform me.

"But she didn't like me drivin' and never bein' back with her at night," Justin said. "It was like, 'Quit drivin' or I leave you.' So I go, 'Bye bye truck.' It wasn't as easy to go, 'Bye bye bottle.' But I had an interview today for a warehouse job."

"What I want to do," Bryna said, "is go to Santa Monica College and study journalism. I want to do ceramics, too."

"If I drank today like I did when I was 17," Justin said, "I'd be dead. I was up to a fifth a day, more some days. I quit drugs a long time ago, but I drank a lot the week we met. She said forget it, so I stopped."

"I never came anywhere near graduating," Bryna said, "but I can get high school courses right at Santa Monica College. Then I can be something. We'll be out of here soon. Our time in the shelter is limited." If this was a declaration, it sounded like a very tentative one, and she followed it with a question. "We won't be here long, will we, Justin?"

"I've still got my health, I know that, and I'm pretty strong," Justin said vaguely, sounding 50 instead of 19. "If I get the ware-house job, I'll be lifting things. Build myself up some more. After that, maybe work in a meat-packing house. I like those big refrigerated rooms where you stay cool all the time. Then I'd like to have my own construction company. Not start at the top, you know, work my way up, start with a hammer and nails. Eventually, you know. Or something else. Whatever. Jesus, I wonder."

"We get his son out here," Bryna said dreamily, without conviction, "there's three of us right there, then we're like a family, aren't we? We get goin' on a home for sure, make it cozy. I don't know. Mobile homes aren't too much, are they? You think I could be a journalist?"

Now she was asking me questions. It was easy enough to reassure Bryna that with study and work she could become a reporter, less easy to reassure myself about her real prospects. I was uncertain whether, without supervision, she could concentrate on any one goal for the length of time it would take her to achieve it. As for supervision, Bryna had long since slipped out of its grasp. There are settlement houses and programs just for teenagers, but it's easy to use them as drop-in and drop-out centers. Once the element of obligation is introduced, as in, "We'd like to have you here, Bryna, but if you stay you have to commit to what we're doing," Brynas tend to drift off. Perhaps Bryna's most realistic prospect, if it can be called that, was in her relationship with Justin. Certainly it was her single source of happiness, and his.

"I slipped up and went out one night three weeks ago," Justin said. "Totally wasted myself. She really let me have it when I came back. We help each other. I guess she helps me more than I help her, don't you baby? Isn't she a sweet one?"

Justin and Bryna were not receiving welfare. They live on handouts from charitable groups they hook up with for a while wherever they happen to find themselves before moving on. I recalled that two of the Chicago teenagers, Rozzy and Merry May, told me they were from families receiving public assistance; Mombasa's and Kenisha's families were not. What none of these adolescents was receiving was preparation for a society that now requires precise skills in exchange for its goods.

The programs that exist to help teenagers are usually extensions of the school system that originally alienated them. It is no harder to elude the programs than the schools. I have concentrated on adolescents who seem already lost because I found so many of them. I also met students in drug rehabilitation programs, remedial education, vocational training, those who don't want to drop out. But the ones I have described here are far more representative of underclass teenagers and of the feelings they expressed to me.

The passivity among underclass youth looks like laziness but masks discouragement. They are windblown through life. In winter they hide, in summer they hang out. They do drop out, they do fall into semipermanent unemployability, they do get pregnant, they do go in and out of jail, they do have drug and alcohol problems that go unattended. AIDS, violence, despair, even suicide are all part of their environment. Death mocks their horizon in a way the middle class does not experience until many decades later. Something crucial has happened, or failed to happen, by the time they are teenagers. This phase of life, so confusing to all of us as we pass through its tests and changes and risks, becomes tragic for the underclass. For the rest of us, these years constitute the long moment when possibility becomes linked with reality. For the underclass, the tragedy is not only that possibility grows further from reality during their adolescence; the tragedy is also that this is when they begin to know it.

Seen from the outside, these teenagers still have the opportunity for growth and change—things will happen to them that are not at all predictable—but they do not know this when they are adolescent members of the underclass. What they know is what they see, and what they see is losing. Because their opportunities are so limited, their real prospects are much less likely to be upward than most of us who are more fortunate can conceive. They are not without resourcefulness, humor, pleasure (especially of the short-term, immediate variety), and plenty of personality. Rozzy in Chicago, Kelso in Bangor, Bryna in Los Angeles clinging to her Justin: all of them contrive to make life yield some form of bounty, some form of love. "He tells me I'm sweet," Bryna said, "but he's the one puts color in my cheeks. Me and him together's the only thing sweet."

I liked them as much as I worried about them. What I wondered, as they headed into the next phase of their lives and I headed away from them, was how all these teenagers were going to cope with maturity. Would they be granted a fresh start somewhere? What is the quality of life that waits for them? Will they achieve security of any kind? What are their chances in the adult society they are about to move into? The teenagers I met are not without yearnings that in more directed circumstances might be called ambition. They are only, in their staggerstep through what passes for youth, without the reasonable expectation of fulfillment that we call hope.

5

Working Hard, Hardly Working

"Lo, the poor poor, yes?" the woman said to me. "Look, the poor aren't who you think they are. They may want what you want and not be able to get it, you know that?" This may have been the most important observation, the most profound lament, I heard during my travels. The remark was made by Adriana Saint Duclos Mathere, who is not a tenured Ivy League sociologist. Her work, when this sad, smiling, still-young mother of two can find it, is packing blueberries or washing dishes in fast-food restaurants. She herself is part of the army of the persistently poor.

Even among those who study poverty or help the disadvantaged find jobs, I met no one who made such an astute comment about the actual wishes of the poor as Adriana Saint Duclos Mathere. She pointed to a simple, obvious, overlooked truth. The poor would like to have what everybody else would like to have. The common middle-class assumption is that character is fate,* and that fate is the residue of will, or lack of will. People who are very poor are widely

---

*This began not as a middle-class assumption but as a literary principle formulated by the decidedly upper-class Aristotle, who tutored Greek royalty, including the future Alexander the Great, before he devoted himself exclusively to philosophy. The notion that character determines destiny is perfectly suited to a society like ours, which wants to believe that virtue—hard work—triumphs.

thought not to care very much. "But of course," Adriana Saint Duclos Mathere said to me, concluding one of our visits, "we care so much! Do you have any idea how difficult it is for the very poor, like me, to find a job—*and* to keep it? Why should this be so?"

In a way I knew why, in a way I didn't.

Because America judges its citizens on how well they can support themselves, I was approaching the heart of my quest. Work forges an essential if almost mystical link between an individual and society. Work was our ancient god even before money or success. Money made you soft. Success was often thought to be a false goal, the attainment of which could hurt others and destroy your own soul. But honest toil was always revered and celebrated above all. I was now ready to see how the underclass works, and does not work. Do the persistently poor see work as something they ought to do, wish they knew how to do, want to avoid, want to learn? Given the deficiencies of preparation among the poorest teenagers I had met, what was I going to find among the next age group?

An intractable quality to poverty in Chicago returned me inevitably to its ghettos. If I looked away, it would be the same as flinching in the face of any other challenge. I felt when I was in Chicago that here was the hardest core, the nucleus with the heaviest particles, the spot where poverty problems and community solutions had most completely melted down. A case in point was the city's many housing projects, where the insight I'd heard applied to San Antonio's Alazan Apache Courts was even more apt: One generation's solution became the next generation's problem. Now that I was looking at work within the underclass, I decided to start in the city that has developed one of the most institutionalized traditions of nonwork. In pursuit of wisdom or even just a theory about what might be done to get the underclass working, while I was on the South Side I went to the University of Chicago to see Professor William Julius Wilson again.

Wilson is the éminence grise of underclass theory. In addition to coining the term "underclass," he has written extensively on the subject; his books include *The Declining Significance of Race* and

The Truly Disadvantaged: The Inner City, the Underclass, and Public Policy. He has tended increasingly to focus on the economic causes of extreme poverty. I wanted to ask him if he saw any hope at all for the vast unemployed adult underclass. Did he share the vision some conjure up of a mass of aberrant, skilless, useless, superfluous people? He did not share that vision, but I couldn't say he cheered me up either. Wilson painted a portrait of a class, almost a separate nation of exiles, who cannot pull themselves up by their bootstraps because they have no boots. "The underclass," Professor Wilson told me, "has a weak attachment to the labor force, a marginal economic position, and lives in an environment that reinforces that weak attachment." Whites, he said, seldom live in these extreme areas of the large cities, which have filled up mostly with the poorest blacks and Hispanics, an underclass that has taken possession of the ghettos at the moment when they have become like emptied shells.

Wilson finds the exterior environment reflected inside underclass households. "There is a correlation between joblessness and family structure," Wilson said. "Employed men are two and a half times more likely to marry the mother of their child. Only 18 percent of ghetto residents have access to an automobile, and if there's no car you can't find a job in the suburbs, where many of the companies have moved. So you're unlikely even to apply for the better-paying job in the suburbs where manufacturing and semiskilled jobs do still exist."

Acknowledging other poverty pockets in small towns and rural areas that are occupied primarily by whites, Wilson, a black sociologist, does not advocate an approach that helps only blacks. "We must open opportunities for poor whites, blacks, and Hispanics," he said. "The programs should be race-neutral—housing subsidies, for instance, to enable people to relocate where jobs are. We need to create jobs, retrain people, move into expanding sectors such as professional services and financial areas. Manufacturing may be down, but wholesale and retail are up. Computer training is needed everywhere. A skilled labor force is essential to the United States' international trade position. A shortage of skilled workers will head up to disaster economically."

In simplest terms, Wilson rejects the idea that the country is dealing with what amounts to a class of bums. From the studies and surveys he has conducted, he sees a lack of opportunity rather than initiative. "The overwhelming majority of jobless want jobs, but if you've been out of work for a long period of time, resignation does set in. After a while you feel your efforts won't pay off. Either you're no good or the world is hostile to you. If you're in the inner city, surrounded by lots of people in the same situation, you develop a collective sense of low self-efficacy. In plain English, you just give up."

My travels so far were quickening my sense of urgency about people Wilson described as having no consistently marketable training. Wanting to see who they were, how they felt, how they survived, I started this phase of my research at the infamous Cabrini-Green projects on the Near North Side. Ted Stokes, an alumnus of Cabrini-Green, was one of my guides around the projects. Though he is not in the underclass, he is not far above it. He might be called a member of the occasionally employed poor who teeters on the brink of the underclass. His diligence and efficiency as a guide were obvious; his grooming and eager, observant eyes under a gently curved forehead help give him exactly the sort of demeanor middle-class employers say they look for. He is alert, sensitive, helpful. Still, he is essentially untrained at any skill that would get him a steady job with possibilities for advancement. When I met him, he had been laid off from his last regular work, at a bakery, for five months. He was drawing unemployment and helping to raise his three children though he had never married their mother and was no longer living with her. "Me and Jolene, we might get back together yet," he said. "Not livin' with the kids is the hardest part."

At 29, Ted Stokes had done carpentry, fencing, plumbing, floor sweeping, dry-walling—"I won't tackle electricity. I mean I know about it but you only get to make one mistake and it's all over"—cleaned lunch rooms, driven a forklift, and served a stint in the Job Corps. He had lost his driver's license a long time ago for leaving the scene of an accident he had caused while he was drunk, but he has never been in major trouble with the police. His brother is a recovering alcoholic, and a brother-in-law died of a heroin overdose. Of another brother-in-law, he says, "Man's a dope fiend, pure and simple; he don't do nothin'. He come in with a hustle and sweep my sister off her feet, but now he just be draggin' her life behind him like a dishtowel. Three kids, and my sister works at an old folks' home, bathin' and feedin' them, to get by."

Since he and Jolene broke up, Ted Stokes has moved back in with his mother, who is housing 14 members of her family on the South Side. In addition to not having his own home as he approached 30, Ted Stokes possessed other components of the underclass profile William Julius Wilson described for me. He can do many odd jobs, but odd jobs no longer add up to a career. Without a car or driver's license, he can't get to the places where the good jobs are even if he were trained to do them. His relationship to his mother's large, self-reliant family was what was holding him above underclass membership. The tenuousness of life in the ghetto is reinforced by the verb Ted Stokes uses when he describes the age of his relatives. "My mother, she made 56 last June." "My brother, he made 35 last year." "My niece is going to make 16 next week." Even 16 is an accomplishment; everyone in the ghetto knows plenty of people who did not "make" 16. Other people make foreman, executive vice president, first string left tackle. In the Chicago ghetto, with luck and pluck, you make 16.

What you don't make much of around Cabrini-Green is money. Ninety percent of the projects' resident's are unemployed. The environment seems destitute of a regenerative vision, beginning with the buildings themselves. The architecture of Cabrini-Green resembles the less enlightened prisons of the '50s. Doorways are gashes cut in the sides of structures that look as if they were initially designed to be subterranean fallout shelters instead of homes. They do not appear to have been conceived with any fondness or even basic human empathy for their prospective inhabitants. Although the projects were once among the most desirable public housing in

Chicago, it was impossible to look at them in the '90s and believe that they were ever intended to do anything for people except get rid of them.

Ted Stokes grew up in Cabrini-Green until he was 12. His cousin, the sociologist Sharon Hicks-Bartlett, accompanying us on part of our tour, lived in the projects for about two years when she was a child. "Cabrini-Green was fun then," she said. "Robberies occasionally, sure, but very seldom violence. Worst thing my group of kids did was throw eggs off the landings." Since then, so many people have thrown so much more than eggs off those landings that they are now wire-meshed. Every open space I saw at the projects is wire-meshed, contributing eerily to the penitentiary look of life there. The more I saw of Cabrini-Green, the less surprising it became that people who live there don't have jobs. Productivity can hardly be the norm where the norm is decay.

At 11:00 A.M., the women we saw on the premises were busy—pushing strollers or carrying laundry—but the men tended to congregate in inert clusters. They looked inert, that is, until I stopped observing at a distance and tried to start a conversation. At one doorway, the young men all scurried away when I asked what they were doing. One of them yelled over his shoulder, "You might be okay, man, but nobody here ain't wanted for something, so everybody gotta stay low."

The elevators were full of urine stench and psychedelic graffiti. The walls carried signs and designs—rainbow swirls like new ice cream flavors, "LORDS CONQUER," a defaced portrait of Malcolm X, a precisely drawn basketball hoop and net, "ROY'S A DEAD MAN," more rainbow swirls. Sharon Hicks-Bartlett thought the graffiti improved the looks of the elevators and corridors. I was less sure. "Sheeeit," was Ted's appreciative comment on the wall art.

On the seventh floor of Sharon's old building, we bumped into a stocky man who looked between 35 and 40, weathered but not much past his prime. Under his Chicago Cubs cap he could have been a veteran outfielder. When he said he was on his way to "an interview," I asked if I could speak to him about jobs he had held. He said sure, he'd show us his home and family, tell us about his work life and his health problems. He described a heart murmur and clogged arteries. "Meet me in my own building, 716 West Division, apartment 907, two o'clock this afternoon. Ask for Ben."

In most of the Cabrini-Green structures there were large blocs of empty apartments. A half-dozen in one spot, a whole floor in another. I stopped counting vacancies when I got up to 100. Ted told me that the other projects he had been to also have numerous vacancies. I couldn't understand how Chicago could have a significant homeless problem, which it does, and also have all these unoccupied apartments in a public housing project. Later, when I asked several officials of the Chicago Housing Authority about this, they gave an explanation that was both reasonable and exasperating. Gangs move into vacant apartments, they said, eventually taking over whole floors. I objected that surely there must be some way to match the supply of apartments with the demand for them. Isn't that the Housing Authority's job?

Indeed, said Katie Kelly, the CHA's external affairs director, the demand is enormous: 44,000 families, meaning between 150,000 and 200,000 individuals, are waiting for public housing in Chicago. Gangs, she said, not only drive families out; they prevent new people from moving in. It was becoming clear to me that a family living in these circumstances needs constant protection and vigilance. A man who leaves his family to look for work or go to a job is a man who might return to find his wife and children terrorized and his property vandalized. Such a man talking to a white stranger like me might well use gang terrorism as an excuse not to work. Six Cabrini-Green women, however, told me virtually the same story. The main reason they wanted their men around was not to be fathers but to be protectors. Three of these women did not in fact have men living with them; their apartments were more frequently vandalized than those of the other three.

Still another CHA official gave me the gang procedure in gutting apartments. Vandals rip out the medicine cabinets that connect the bathrooms. This permits them to crawl through to the next apartment, and the next, until they have made a whole floor their own. They steal the copper tubing used in heating ducts, pull out all metal as well as plumbing fixtures, and render the apartments unusable. Having sold everything they can, they then set up business in the vacant apartments and harass any legitimate tenant who stays. I heard these complaints from Cabrini-Green residents as well. The only difference between descriptions by CHA officials and Cabrini-Green residents was that the former blamed the gangs while the latter blamed both the gangs and the slow-moving CHA.

Cabrini-Green, which has 3,500 apartments, was only two-thirds filled when I visited it and therefore could have been home to well over 1000 of the 44,000 waiting families. Katie Kelly explained that Housing Authority officials conduct "sweeps" in which they go from apartment to apartment, floor to floor, inspecting each unit and its maintenance needs. "We try to keep the gangs on the move," she said, "but when we fix up a building, they go across the street, and when we go across the street, they move down the block. When we follow them down the block, they jump to another block, and we follow them there eventually. As soon as residents see some security come to a development, things get significantly better. But all this takes time and money."

The Housing Authority is in the process of putting guards in the lobbies along with high-security locks, such as those I passed through to get to the Beethoven Project in the Robert Taylor Homes. When there are several vacancies on a floor, the Housing Authority moves the rest of the tenants to a lower floor, seals off the vacant one, and begins the process of renovating it. With several upper floors sealed off, the empty look is worse than it would be if the Housing Authority simply left every family in place scattered around the building. But leaving tenants in place opens a floor with vacancies to the gangs and vandals. When the Housing Authority pays attention, most residents are glad to have the increased security. The problem, of course, is that families don't like to be moved around like ciphers, buildings acquire a bombed-out Beirutish look that is demoralizing, and the whole process of fixing the vacant apartments takes a scandalously long time due to budget restrictions.

The new security systems in the projects make them look like a jumbled hybrid of upscale New York East Side coops and the Rikers Island prison. The sophisticated security can make people feel incarcerated in their own homes even as it protects them from unwanted outsiders, and sometimes from desired visitors. Most of the tenants I talked to felt there still wasn't enough security and wanted to see more. I heard predictable stories about a security guard accused of rape, a lobbyman who deals drugs. The bottom line is hardly news: The system works if those who run it work. Three hundred apartments had recently been brought back into use in Cabrini-Green, but 1,200 remained empty. The vacancies—some windows broken, others boarded up—gave the buildings faces that appeared to have had many of their teeth knocked out.

When Ted Stokes and I found our way to the apartment building where Ben, the stocky man with the heart murmur and the Chicago Cubs cap, told us to meet him, Ted refused to enter it. A larger than usual clutch of idle men had gathered around the downstairs entrance in early afternoon. Having grown up in Cabrini-Green, Ted said he knew this building was a bad one, a combat zone. "Not one side or the other controls it, and it's full of drugs. Everybody be fightin' over it, lookin' for what they can get."

Naively, I urged Ted on until he finally agreed to go into the building, which he would not let me enter by myself. Once inside, our concern was only to get to Ben's apartment as quickly as possible. I'd never seen more distinctly, more unambiguously, more maddeningly, the results of the poverty policy gridlock in America. The urine in the corridors smelled sharper, older; the graffiti images were more violent; the elevator was completely inoperable, a relic of itself. The building had lost the demarcations that separate the usage of one space from the usage of another: People slept in the lobby, defecated in the stairwell, threw garbage into hallways. I was least prepared for the vomit Ted and I barely avoided stepping in. Navigating jerkily

past dingy heaps of humans and human waste, I fought to keep my
own junkfood lunch in my stomach. In the shadows I didn't really
want to know whether it was feces or a used condom I slipped on. As
we picked our way up the last dark staircase, I understood how
completely everyone has dropped the social ball with respect to the
underclass: liberals, conservatives, labor, business, black leaders,
white leaders, the poor themselves. None of us had treated the
existence of an underclass as a problem, with the result that it
became a crisis. At this point there could be no mistaking the reality
that the underclass is now a crisis and a trauma for our whole society.
I was angry, ashamed, discouraged. But at the same time, I was
determined to get in and out of Ben's apartment as fast as possible.

"Dono any Ben around here," said a large-breasted, red-
sweatered lady, not happy about seeing two strangers outside her
door. She slammed the door in our faces. Ted and I were considering
what to do next when the door opened again. A tan-sweatered, taller
woman, also with an ample bosom, came out holding the hand of a
corn-curled little girl. "Yeah, I know Ben. Where is the son of a b?"
That was what we wanted to know. I explained quickly about my
book, and she went on. "Well, I know Ben. I had a baby with Ben,
but Ben's not here." She stroked the shoulder of the corn-curled little
girl, who looked to be about three. I asked if Ben lived there. "No, my
sister lives here. I'm just visiting. She don't like Ben. Ben lives in
Kankakee. You see him in that other Cabrini building on North
Larrabee? I didn't know he's still keeping company with that girl
over there. The son of a b." End of visit. Go figure. Why did Ben tell
us to meet him at the apartment of his former girlfriend's sister who
doesn't like him? Was the little corn-curled girl Ben's? Was there any
reason why the former girlfriend should bother telling us anything
other than the answers that would protect her? Was Ben, figuring us
for agents of the state one way or another, hiding in the apartment
while we chatted outside it, still at his other girlfriend's place, on his
way to Kankakee?

You can't count the Bens in Chicago. They have all kinds of
medical problems, whether self-inflicted, job-related, or produced by

the conditions they are born into. In that sense, they are hardly cheating if they receive public assistance. I saw many other Bens at a South Side soup kitchen set up in the basement of a church. Some of their talk was from the heart; some was bottle-fed or needle-induced.

Baron Sampson was typical of the 100 or so men having lunch in the First Presbyterian Church basement the day I was there. He described the scars on his cheeks and eyelids as coming from a car accident, a knifing, and a mistake he made by trying to weld without wearing goggles. Wearing only a thin corduroy jacket against the icy air sweeping off Lake Michigan, he was picking at his stringbeans, one at a time, making them last as long as he could. Sampson has served three and a half years at Stateville for armed robbery. "What I did, I robbed a liquor store and somebody told on us. Now I'm just lazy. Thirty-one years old and don't have the price of a cussword. Left two women with three kids, haven't seen any of them since I walked out of the pen. This place closes, I'm gonna go score me a Canadian Club." Planless, powerless, and ashamed, he lurked for a while, watching suspiciously while I listened to a dozen others, then shuffled off to find a stiff drink against the cold wind.

What do we say to a man like Baron Sampson? The hell with you? You don't have my sympathy on moral, religious, or aesthetic grounds? Off you go, Buddy, see you later in the heap of unreclaimable poor? Or do we hope some born-againers scoop him up? He's a young man, he's no longer young, he ought to be working, he's not working, he ought to be doing *something*, he's not doing anything. Baron Sampson in his shame seems so broken that even a well-executed crime would be a boost for his opinion of himself. I have used the word "shame" here more than once because I felt it myself and I felt it around me. Shame even has its own smell, the smell of being used up too soon, chronically humiliated, desperate no longer for improvement, desperate only to disappear.

To stop feeling this way, I turned to violence. From the Presbyterian church I went a few blocks west to a building where young men practice the one sport where the goal is to hurt your opponent so badly he can no longer practice the sport. In the murky South

Side gym in a neighborhood where many buildings have been torched, a man sparred by himself, shadow boxing. He was a junior middleweight named Billy Oakes who has already thrown one leg over the invisible fence around the ghetto, a pro with a nine and two record. The gym in the slums has a quality of resonance because of its fixed position in American legend. The tough mick, wop, kike, spic, nigger fighting his way out of his background. Now if the kid can only stay upright. Billy Oakes trained hard. He had a jab that was heartening if you weren't on its receiving end. He moved well. He did not appear to have much of a right. Inside, the work is brutal and he succeeds only by making someone else fail. Outside, those Billy Oakes is trying to leave behind throw dice, get wasted, shoot up, hit each other, make babies, stand around, wait.

Mostly, they do not work. I was looking for workers here, those of working age in the underclass. I was finding some who work hard, but more who hardly work. However far outside the American mainstream they may be, this was discouraging, plainly, to my subjects because work remains the standard by which most of us, including the underclass, judge ourselves. But as my quest proceeded, the almost countless members of the nonworking underclass were also discouraging to me.

Organizations and agencies do exist to try to put the underclass to work, as I saw in many places, but these reach only a tiny slice of the persistently poor who need them. The need is geometrically greater than the sources of help. Lacking broad support, these sources continually fight a battle for mere survival. Such sources—the agencies that help the poor—are generally without noisy constituencies. The potential beneficiaries, the underclass themselves, are far removed from a position to serve as their own advocates in the way manufacturers or teamsters or the elderly do. The result is that the helping agencies mirror the experience of those they are set up to help. As a group, the underclass is perhaps that branch of society most left to fend for itself and least able to do so.

There are always disadvantaged individuals who do pull themselves up, and some of these find their calling afterward at the helping agencies themselves. Franklin Jones, head of the Parent Child Center in Chicago, comes from a family on public assistance. His father died when he was two, his mother worked as a maid, and he was a high school dropout. "My mother got mad at me," he said, "pushed me back into school. I had a lot of kin, people who called me brother, and that helped when I was growing up without a father." His three brothers and one sister each worked all the time, and all made the leap to middle-class and solid working-class comfort.

Rodney Pippit is a fresh-faced 32-year-old Chicagoan, also from the South Side, with a background even more deprived than Franklin Jones'. Eager for any job he can find, he works the lobby and elevators in a Lake Shore Drive building. But this is only the beginning of his workday. He does a second shift in another building as a garbage man. That's 16 hours a day. Then he repairs refrigerators and television sets in his own building. Weekends he is a car mechanic in his South Side neighborhood except on Sunday morning, when he takes time to preach in his own small church. "You got to have a gratitude attitude," he said when I asked him how he stays on his feet. With five children, Rodney Pippet is not, he had to admit, making it. He is, however, very proud he's not on the dole. "Keep pumping," he said, "till you get someplace you want to be." If Baron Sampson, the scarcely functioning derelict I met in the Presbyterian church basement, can be multiplied 1,000 times in the Chicago ghetto, so can Rodney Pippit. The problem is, the Baron Sampsons are so demoralized by the time they reach their mid-20s they see no way to turn themselves into the Rodney Pippets.

Wherever I went I looked for whatever kind of help was available. When I found it, the help was always heartening even when it appeared to be drastically less than what begged to be done. Sometimes what looked to be almost a genetic implant was being woven into an individual, as at Demicco Youth Services in Chicago. This is an organization that attempts to put work on the horizon of people who do not come from work traditions. I had forgotten, perhaps never realized, how each of us has an understanding with society, whether we are confident or fearful, in which we have certain benefits, rights, expectations, obligations, accountability. Because the underclass does not feel covered by this understanding, the link to the larger group, the link that makes work both possible and necessary, hasn't been forged for them. The process of joining an individual to society might seem elementary and obvious; it is also urgent and indispensable. For most of us, the process is fairly complete by the time we are in early adolescence. For the underclass, frequently lacking families and structures that incorporate work, the slow accretion of responsibility and self-esteem may not begin until an individual is fully grown—if it ever begins at all.

Representatives of Demicco Youth Services, which helps young adults learn how to get and keep jobs, showed me what they refer to as character building among those whose emotional deprivation has been as severe as their unmet material needs. Under a contract from the Chicago mayor's office to recruit ghetto residents into employability, Demicco's staff promotes the work ethic to counteract what Professor Wilson described to me as the "weak attachment to the labor force" among the underclass. They begin by teaching those who have seldom worked how to go to a job interview. Showing up on time, looking the personnel manager in the eye, a firm handshake: Habits ingrained in the middle class are new experiences for the underclass. Lengthy training sessions use role reversal techniques so that prospective employees will temporarily become their own prospective bosses. They can see what they look like, how they come off, to someone trying to run a business.

Watching a role reversal, I thought it might be valuable if employers, too, were schooled in the point of view of the job applicant whose principal qualification is need. "I know where you're coming from," a would-be employee said to the role-playing boss near the end of a training interview, "but you have no idea, man, where I'm coming from." Emphasizing pride and discipline among those with no tradition of either, the Demicco trainers try to change the course of a young life before it is irretrievably lost in terms of productivity. When I visited Demicco, the organization had recently sponsored a job fair to bring together tenants of Cabrini-Green with potential employers. The agency invited 100 Chicago companies to the fair. Fifteen came, including First National Bank, Federal Express, and AT&T. The year before, Demicco had placed 176 people in jobs, and 80 percent were still working when I was there. A small, struggling, underfunded good idea, Demicco reaches perhaps 1 percent of the people who need it.

After Ted Stokes and I had completed a long day in the ghetto, I was famished. I would shortly be leaving for Oakland, again looking for people who were looking for work. Or not bothering to look. The day had been draining, and my prospect was, at best, uncertain. I wanted to forget for a while what the underclass was up against, and what I was up against in trying to be their chronicler. Because the ghetto left me feeling hollow and depleted, I supposed it had that effect on Ted Stokes, too. Glad for his company, I invited Ted to dinner, not as some kind of reward (I was paying him), but to share an antidote to misery, deprivation, corruption, decay, and hunger itself.

I'd forgotten that I was the recruit in this situation, Ted the drill sergeant used to 30-mile marches. He declined dinner, saying he wanted to pick up his seven-year-old daughter, and accepted only a McDonald's pitstop where he had two quick fish filets and a Mcsalad. His cousin, Sharon Hicks-Bartlett, far more used to the ghetto than I but far less than Ted, was also hungry after our Cabrini-Green visit had given her an unaccustomed plunge back toward her beginnings. The two of us replenished ourselves at the most elegant Italian restaurant in Chicago. She had risotto with calamari, scallops, and shrimp, while I had swordfish in a soy and ginger marinade, blanketed with black olives, accompanied by an arugula and endive salad misted with a raspberry vinaigrette dressing. I was glad of the escape, as hungry for this setting as I was for the meal itself. Yet I did not so easily escape the incongruity between my evening and the day that led to it. The service, the scene, the elaborately prepared meal all reminded me how hard it is to understand what life would be like with no access to comforts like these, the multitudes of cozily assumed luxuries, large and small, which I enjoy. No one I met throughout the long day, of

course, would have had the slightest chance to leap out of his or her life
into this dinner. The gulf between my subjects and me widened again.

The kind of work the underclass does most faithfully is the work of
simply surviving. Survival without training or money requires a
dogged diligence and jungle alertness that the middle class is likely to
exercise only as a lark, however worthwhile, in a program such as
Outward Bound. A former food merchant was the first Oakland
citizen I met, a baker who was, like me, watching schoolchildren
through a cyclone fence. I had come upon Jeremy Holland during my
pursuit of underclass children. He had told me then, almost as
an introduction while we watched children in a school playground,
that he had killed a man. This was not delivered menacingly but
plaintively, as though the killing were Jeremy Holland's misfortune
nearly as much as his victim's. He hung out at a neighborhood pizza
joint in West Oakland and told me I could find him there most
afternoons if he wasn't working.

The next time I was in Oakland I found Jeremy Holland at the
pizza joint as surely as if we'd had an appointment. He finished his
beer, stuck an Oakland A's cap on his head, and we walked through
the neighborhood he'd returned to, on and off, all his life. "Draws
me back, the old plantation, no matter how far I roam," he said as we
passed battered old houses that still had friendly stoops with kids
playing on them. His reference to a plantation was both sentimental
and ironic; it was what he had for a past. "Plus I can generally get me
a job of some kind of work here."

Jeremy Holland is a short, wiry, middle-aged man, able to pivot
easily on his feet, on which he wears beat-up Nike running shoes. His
face looked traveled. It could have been a roadmap of the west,
displaying his 15 years in Colorado and Arizona, his Los Angeles
decade, his return to Oakland six years ago. Yet only his eyes looked
tired. The rest of him was still ready for any shift of fortune. He
wasn't working steadily now, having been fired from his last job, as a
cake and pie baker, for hitting his foreman with a mixing paddle.

Though he had also been an upholsterer off and on for 30 years, he hadn't been able to land that kind of work lately. But he still did pickup jobs, and he was not looking for handouts. "I'm not on welfare because I got my *pride,* man," Jeremy Holland said. "I do odds and ends for people, fix a car here, paint a fence there, pick up bottles and cans and turn them in. It is not necessary to be humiliated for $200, $300 a month from welfare."

This man who described himself as having too much pride for welfare had also been convicted of murder. He saw no contradiction. It may have been his pride that cost him his last job. As Jeremy Holland tells it, the foreman in the pastry kitchen knew he had done a stretch in San Quentin for murder. The foreman never let up on Jeremy Holland about his record, and he didn't like black people anyway. "I'd been at the bakery over four years," Holland said, "when I hit him with the paddle after all his harassing. They said go home and cool off. The next morning they told me to get my check— in other words, see ya later. End of job."

He did not feel shortchanged by life. "When I was young and care-free, I kept doing crazy things. Burglaries, a few assaults. Finally I effed up but good. Killed a drug dealer while I was robbing him. I don't carry a gun anymore, just this little bitty knife." He pulled it out and flicked open the switchblade, smiling as if to offer its services.

Looking down at his beat-up sneakers, Jeremy Holland pulled his torn jacket tighter around him and tugged at his baseball cap, musing on his life and the life he had taken. "Killing the guy has given me night-mares. Thirteen years and I still wake up sweating it out. He had a kid; drug dealers have kids too. Disgraced my own family, no question about that. My parents were good people, poor as nails, but good. I had a twin brother, Ivan, who died at birth. Wonder what he'd been like. My mother always talked about him like he just went away and would come back. My father worked hard all his life. He died while I was in San Quentin. We live old in my family, and I'm just a young 54. I don't know what I'm going to do. I'd like to do something."

The Jeremy Hollands do not merely slip through cracks in social programs; by the time they are middle-aged they have long since fallen out of society altogether. And yet Jeremy Holland wanted work. He did not know where he was going to find it, but he wanted it. A few blocks away, leaning against a sidewalk stoop, the next man I met in Oakland was a younger version of Jeremy Holland, also a convicted killer. Tall and hulking, Eric Blyden, 30, was raised in an East Oakland neighborhood where, he said, "It was easier to get dope than work. This other dude takes my car after we partied. Brings it back all banged up. I was still high. I wasted him."

Blyden did a drum roll of the prisons he has been in as if these formed a pedigree. "San Quentin, Folsom, Tracy, Mule Creek State, Soledad, Vacaville, California Men's Colony in San Luis Obispo— I've seen 'em all." Hovering over his group of buddies, Eric Blyden watched as they scattered when I asked if any of them was currently working. "We all done time, none of us got a job," he told me, "yet and still street life don't work either. I mean to try for some help." He did not specify the kind of help he wanted. When I asked what kind, he drooped, his chin almost touching his chest. "Drugs, you know, man." He was mumbling. "Get me clean, get me some computer training, I get me a job, you dig?" It is necessary to go three generations back in Eric Blyden's family to find someone who even has a home. When I met him he was staying with his grandmother.

Yet a third Oakland street man, a friend of Eric Blyden called only Abu, chanted his own prisons: San Quentin, Folsom, Susanville, on and on. He did get odd jobs doing sheetrocking, plumbing, warehousing, installing electrical appliances. But Abu said he has never had steady work, and he seems to hold his jobs in between his crimes rather than vice versa.

Finally, I met a young man with a career, a trainee plumber apprenticed to his uncle. Barry Knight was working six days a week. He has been in trouble, he said, "but never to the pen." Clear-eyed and slope-shouldered, with an Afro he kept combing, he had been more committed to an education than any of the others I spoke to during my prowl among the Oakland underclass. He did not quit school until he was shot in a fight during 12th grade. Unlike the others, who were pleasant and at ease, Barry Knight was hostile and surly. "Why should I believe that you believe that I can make it where my friends don't?" he shot at me. Because he has drive, that was why. The apprentice plumber scoffed at his friends, at life on the street, at my questions. "Shut your face, I shut it for you," he replied when I asked about his family. "Background, man? Yeah, right. Well, my dad's an ex-pimp, retired now, I've seen him three times in my life. Beautiful, right?" This led me to think that his anger may be the positive force propelling him into a professional status his friends lacked. Barry Knight was reading my mind. "I may not be famous for my sweetness, you hear, but I'm not going to be asking the man for my spending money."

Except for Barry Knight, the street life of these men seemed as important to them as work, if not more important. The social contacts of the workplace were unavailable to them. Among these underclass men, their water cooler and coffee maker are the street corners and sidewalks where they meet daily. This street life was essentially a men's club. Few women, and never the women they had special involvements with, hung around with the men during the day. Among underclass women I found different routines and schedules, different sets of tasks and responsibilities.

First and last for underclass women, there are children, always children, providing a relief from the burden of poverty yet also contributing to that burden more mightily than anything else in the women's lives. Children limit their underclass mothers' educational, professional, and economic opportunities. I had already seen, everywhere I went, the almost total responsibility for children borne by underclass women. Whether they discharge the responsibility in ways the middle class would approve or not, it is a task seldom shared with men. (Ted Stokes in Chicago was an exception, but he wasn't exactly in the underclass either.) I wanted to know if child rearing left persistently poor women time for other work, or even time to look for other work.

Irma Adkins is a West Oakland neighborhood resident who was

once on welfare and now works as a therapeutic foster parent. Knowing the turf, she said, she would send me to an underclass woman admired locally as a success story. "Ronnielee's a reclamation project unto herself," she said, "and people around the 'hood are making book on whether she can pull it off." A beige colored black woman in her 40s, Irma Adkins was working hard to buy the once-elegant Victorian house she was renting. It was both run-down and full of potential for the restoration she wanted to give it. If she became able to buy it, as she wanted to do, it would be the first piece of property she had ever owned. Meanwhile, she was raising a foster child and still providing much of the support for her own three nearly grown daughters. She received virtually no help from their three different fathers, two of whom she had married.

While she swam furiously every day against a California economic undertow that pulled down the semiskilled, she also struggled to help others. If doing a fair share can be quantified, Irma Adkins is an example of a type of woman who does considerably more. I thought about our cultural inhibitions against giving such women the credit, both emotional and economic, they are due. Inevitably, we don't give them that credit because it would involve condemnation of the men who impregnate and desert them.

A block away from Irma Adkin's house, the neighborhood success story, identified only as Ronnielee, was said to have kicked her cocaine habit and to be training for a job. She was bringing up her five children with no help from a man. I went to her house twice when she was out and then, through an employee of the Jubilee West agency, was able to make an appointment with her. Ronnielee did not show up for the appointment. Was she looking for work? Strung out?

I went around to Irma Adkins' house. She thought it was possible Ronnielee had taken a few hits. "It's tough out there," she said. "You may slide back. You don't get cured all at once." Irma sat in a tan wicker fanback chair; light-skinned, she almost blended into her background. She wanted to adopt the foster child she was currently caring for even though her income is low and will be lower still after she loses the foster parent stipend. But she preferred the closeness of an adoption to the less binding, less personal arrangement of foster parenthood. She hoped to get a housing grant available to first-time homeowners so she could buy her house. "It's what I need at this point in my life—a child, a home of my own. We need to belong to each other. We *need* that so much." The urgency of what she said, the sincerity in her voice, moved me. Yet she also had trouble sitting still, and she kept reaching for things she had no use for at the moment—a paperweight, a quill pen, a jar of cold cream, two books. The uneasiness in Irma Adkins' manner proclaimed her own neediness, which was at least the equal of her foster child's.

On my fourth visit to Ronnielee's home, I at last met her. With high cheekbones and a proud bearing, she is a 38-year-old, dark-skinned Jamaican who is quick to smile nervously. She introduced herself as Ronnielee Divine, eagerly adding that she formerly worked as a clerk typist as well as a nurse's aide. "I lost one of my babies to crib death while I was working as a nurse's aide," she said. "My husband was very abusive and was no help with our three-year-old who has sickle cell anemia. That's when I started to take coke." She opened a commercial advertising service, losing it primarily because of cocaine and its own economically marginal nature. Now she was taking a child development class and a course in bookkeeping, though she never graduated from high school. Ronnielee's hands moved constantly as she spoke, often fluttering through her hair. She was clearly jittery, desperate to be approved of, and I felt very intrusive.

Ronnielee Divine insisted on showing me around her apartment, which has a lot of space—"I need four bedrooms because I got me a barrel of kids"—but almost no furniture. The living room was picked up and neat, but the other rooms all had children's dirty clothing on the floor. Not so different from suburbia except the clothes were cheaper and the rooms had beds but no chairs in them. Her 19-year-old son was lying on his bed in the middle of the day, polite but supine. She was proud of him for having earned a high school diploma despite having severe dyslexia.

"I'll work again," Ronnielee said, "I know I will. Child welfare took my kids from me once on the coke thing, never more. Oh, I'll snitch me a beer now and then, don't tell anyone, but I'm climbing the ladder. In five years I'll have me an advertising business." She laughed anxiously.

I asked Ronnielee Divine what she liked about drugs.

"Well, drugs are a *thrill,* excuse my French, they're a *climax.* But drugs landed me with pneumonia and gave me all the trouble I've had. I'm going to keep up with my nursing, too, advertising and nursing. It's a striving time, but I'll come through. You know I'll make it, don't you?"

"Sure," I said, though of course I couldn't tell about Ronnielee Divine. Her own friend and booster, Irma Adkins, had said she might not be finished with drugs, but she was so determined to pull herself up, so full of plans, I hated to come to that conclusion. Her goals were not unrealistic; they were attainable with effort and stamina. But they were also, it seemed to me, largely the product of fright at the thought of having her children taken from her again. Hoping that encouragement might help, I gave her more reassurance than I felt her prospects warranted. Ronnielee shares certain circumstances I found among the most hopeful of the underclass women I met. Even those with considerable professional ambition face towering obstacles and are plagued by crippling insecurities and problems—lack of education, a violent spouse, too many children they have to raise by themselves, drugs, alcohol.

Unable to make up my mind about Ronnielee Divine, I walked back around to see Irma Adkins. The first thing I noticed when she opened her door was that her ornate Victorian house was suffused with marijuana smoke. I asked about it. Irma Adkins took a deep breath and smiled benignly. She was relaxed now. "That's my healing," she said.

I was missing some point here. Both women have pain. They are not merely victims—their pain is not inflicted exclusively from without by males or by society—but victimization is an element in their lives. And this pain is not about drugs. With both Irma Adkins and Ronnielee Divine, respectively representing the working poor and the underclass, there is the unspoken plea: I've raised my kids, done what I'm supposed to do. When does the good part start, or even just when does my turn start? For these women the doubts, fears, and precariousness never let up; they don't get comfort time, they don't have any margin for error. Everything they do must either help them up or keep them down. Irma Adkins is trying to hang onto middle-class trappings more or less provided by the state. Ronnielee Divine is trying to hang onto her children more or less taken from her by the state. She is also trying to move herself up a notch through her dreams of betterment, dreams of *self*-betterment to be precise. She is not looking for a free ride; she wants to achieve her goals on her own. That's the only way Ronnielee knows how to feel better about herself. "It's a striving time," she said. Even as "cases" the two women are poignant, not only sad but hopeful, each blueprinting her future, each on the verge of things if only things can be coaxed into working out.

My experiences in Los Angeles and San Antonio underscored the conditions I found in Chicago and Oakland. Many of the faces I saw in the coastal sections of Los Angeles were white, most in San Antonio were brown. In downtown Los Angeles, away from the beaches, the poor are black, white, and Hispanic, often frequenting different flophouses and soup kitchens according to their background, staying more in their own neighborhoods in the fashion of other large cities. As Newton observed, however, falling objects in a vacuum descend at the same rate of acceleration. When they have nothing to hang onto and nothing to catch them, they enter a free-fall state, and their color is as irrelevant as their weight.

Southern California used to draw migrants to its almost perennially growing economy, its gentle climate, and the sense of limitless possibility it represented to those unacquainted with its harsher realities. Whether they fled the Oklahoma Dustbowl in the '30s or the Northeast rustbelt in the '80s, refugees always hoped to find a new start in sunny California. But then the defense budget declined, the oil industry went into a tailspin, and the computer business recessed. News of the collapse of the California job market in the early '90s traveled slowly among the unemployed, however. "People still come out here thinking they'll find jobs more easily," an unemployment office claims processor told me in Santa Monica, "but that isn't true anymore. If workers arrive and don't find jobs right away, they can't even qualify for unemployment. It's a short ride from the steady low-paying jobs they had before to the breadlines." She was raising the issue of those on the brink of extreme poverty, on the brink of the underclass itself. They have too much education, and a background of too much employment, to qualify for inclusion in William Julius Wilson's underclass, but their suffering is as genuine, their prospects as bleak, their need for remedial help almost as unfulfilled.

One of the claims processor's clients was a 56-year-old maintenance man who had moved to California from Florida three months earlier. I talked to him about where he had been economically and where he saw himself heading. Tall but stooped, gray, and sagging everywhere, Sam Wheeler was a sketch, and an embodiment, of free fall itself. He even used a similar metaphor. "No place to go but up," he said, "only I can't figure out where 'up' is located, so I keep going the other way." After arriving in Los Angeles, he had found no job and soon had to give up his new apartment to move in with his sister. He went on interviews at schools, apartment complexes, office buildings, all of which had job openings. Nobody hired him. "I been doing maintenance work all my life," he told me. "I can fix anything that's broke. I thought experience was supposed to count for something, but no one wants a new guy who's 56." Sam Wheeler was not in the underclass, but he was heading in its direction and saw no way to break his fall. He now felt as discarded as he had recently felt hopeful when he migrated from Florida. "My sister's apartment is in Santa Monica, not far from the beach," he said wearily. "I wake up some mornings, stroll down there, and feel like the best thing is just to keep on going right into the ocean and don't look back."

A few blocks west of the unemployment office where I spoke to Sam Wheeler, California's contrasts became starkly physical. Along

the beguiling Palisades Park in Santa Monica, a palm-lined prom-
enade overlooking the Pacific, I saw people in agonizing need pushed
up against the end of the continent. They walked aimlessly along the
path at the top of the ocean-fronting cliff; many didn't even bother to
beg. At night they stopped walking and curled up in bedrolls, if they
had them, and tried to sleep. A young widower was more desperate
than most of the others. He had come out from Pennsylvania to work
in a soft-drink bottling factory, but that job had evaporated. He was
now begging in order to support his two small daughters, whom he
had left temporarily with their aunt in the San Fernando Valley.
Without transportation or money, in the neighborhoods he had
walked around no one even wanted him as a handyman. Scraggly,
disheveled, and unwashed, he could not have made a particularly
appealing job seeker. For whatever it was worth, he was sober.
He had tried to get work as a mechanic, but he was told at several
garages that there were many more competent mechanics in Los
Angeles than there were openings for them. "My little girls can only
stay with my sister a few more days," he said, "and I have to find
something or I'll lose them. When my wife died I went to hell. Don't
use my name and don't embarrass me, please. If she saw me today,
she'd die again."

I paused to take stock of these working-age nonworkers and of
my response to them. Their misery was general, in so many places I
had traveled around America, from Maine where I now live to southern California where I was born. I felt at different times in the presence of these poorest poor: Sympathy; pity (unhelpful, sentimental);
thankfulness I'm not them; heightened senses of sight, taste, smell;
the dull, rigid, clinical, blocked-off lack of sensation that surgeons
and private investigators have to give themselves while they are
operating; fear for my physical safety; fear for my emotional condition; desire to flee; desire to stay forever not so much to help as to
understand better and tell about what I saw; also desire to help; the
urge to shout about them (not simply write or explain or "communicate" their condition) to anyone who would listen and to grab by the
lapels anyone who wouldn't; hopelessness (why bother telling about

them when no one's going to do anything anyway?); anger at some vague entity called "society"; anger at the underclass themselves (why are you there, why don't you pull yourselves up, why don't you leave me alone, why don't you become invisible again, why don't you blow away?); haunted, as at a permanent seance.

A calibrated scream would possibly have been the best way to handle these feelings. But I kept trying to uncover some secret that might become a solution; some realization, some key insight that would make sense of all my wonderings and wanderings. I put the scream aside, or perhaps I incorporated it. As I stood one day on the palisades in Santa Monica, scrutinizing the very, very poor as they transacted their business of bare survival, I found myself in the rabid fantasy that I was becoming them. You are what you see. Instead of emitting my scream, I decided to look like them.

Being white, I thought it was more appropriate to try blending in with my deep-poverty surroundings in a predominantly white area. I wanted to experience what the very poor experience when they look as they do. Would I be shunned? Offered help? I also wanted to see how the poor themselves would treat me. Would they trust me more? Respect me less? In Chicago, Oakland, or San Antonio, I simply would have been spotted as an outsider in a ghetto or barrio, the same as when I wore my usual clothes. In Maine, where the persistently poor are generally white, I had already made friends at the local shelter and soup kitchen by the time I thought of becoming a vagrant, so it didn't make sense to try to disguise myself the next time I turned up in Bangor. Anyway, I was already in California. My first hometown, Santa Monica, so close to the world capital of make-believe, became, ironically, the one place where I pretended to be someone I'm not.

Posing as a homeless person newly arrived in southern California, I tried to find various kinds of help around Santa Monica. I stopped shaving for several days, wore a torn shirt, took the lace out of one of my shoes and broke the lace in the other shoe so it was tied unevenly. Smudging my face with dirt, I thought I looked too much like the self-consciously made-up actors in the movie version of *The Grapes of*

Wrath, so I rubbed it off. The rest was easy. In the already somewhat vagabond setting of the beach neighborhood, I was accepted readily. As I stepped into my role I was too intent on my experiment, and I'd already been around the very poor too long, to feel awkward. But the very first day, after losing 50 cents in a black jack game underneath the Santa Monica pier, I walked right into a situation that threatened to blow my cover.

As I emerged from the overhanging pier into the sunlight of the walking track along the beach, I bumped into a fashionably dressed high school classmate I hadn't seen in over 30 years. Rolex, Lacoste, Gucci. This was a jovial fellow I'll call Andy, once an immovable football center, a dogged debater, and a decent right fielder. His father had been a successful Chevrolet dealer. I started to smother my embarrassment with an explanation when it struck me that this would be more interesting if I simply let him have his own reaction to a classmate fallen on hard times.

It turned out Andy was a lot more embarrassed than I was. After the briefest exchange—"What the hell happened to you?" "It's a long story . . . "—Andy reached into his pocket. I was considering whether I ought to accept his money when what he put into my waiting hand was a business card. Advertising, public relations, speechwriting. Kind of a free-lance image maker himself. He probably could have advised me on a shrewder disguise than the one I'd adopted. "See if there's anything I can do. Tough luck. Give me a call at the office." Did I detect a slight let's-keep-this-guy-at-arm's-length emphasis on "at the office?" Andy started off but couldn't resist turning around to lob a dollop of long-held wisdom at me. "You know, I always said it was a mistake to go East to college." In the next issue of our alumni news, however, Andy protected me; there was no mention of our encounter.

For the rest of my week's impersonation of a man in deep poverty, although I found myself being treated far less well than normally, I was not mistreated either. But there was a notable lack of accuracy in most of what passed for the information that I was given. This information came from both the middle class and my fellow vagrants. I had the impression that going undercover had not put me in touch with reality so much as with vagueness. Indeed, vagueness *was* the new reality. That, of course, conveys its own level of truth, as well as its own problem.

The people I asked for instructions on where to find various services for the needy were courteous, but they were astonishingly misinformed. For food distribution, a shelter, and the unemployment office, I was repeatedly given a succession of wrong addresses by police officers, parks department employees who deal every day with the homeless, and once by an official on the steps of the Santa Monica City Hall. Even with a rented car parked a handy few blocks from wherever I did my questioning, I became discouraged. If a policeman couldn't tell me where the welfare office was, why bother to keep looking for it? When a needy person has marginal literacy, no car, and three hungry children in tow, a wrong address can lead to a quick surrender. A number of the wandering poor told me similar stories of misinformation. Regardless of where the misinformation comes from, it is plainly discouraging to a person, perhaps somewhat disoriented anyway, who is unfamiliar with his or her surroundings. After a few wrong turns in the search for a shelter, an individual or a family will give up and sleep under a bridge or a freeway overpass; or they don't persevere in applying for the unemployment or welfare benefits they are legally entitled to.

Looking more like the people whose lives I was trying to understand did not seem to change their attitudes toward me as much as I had thought it might. Most had not acted wary or intimidated before, nor did they become dramatically more friendly now when I showed up in the kinds of clothing they themselves wore. I was still asked for cigarettes in my poverty drag, but now I was also offered cigarette butts. I did find out how generous underclass people can be. It's true the persistently poor sometimes rob one another, especially when drugs are involved, but in my experience they are far more likely to share their meager belongings than the middle and upper middle classes are. In addition to cigarette butts, I was offered bottles of 7-Up and Pepsi Cola, swigs of wine, full cans of beer, halves of sandwiches, pieces of fruit, shoelaces (for my unlaced shoe), a couple of half-joints of marijuana, a sweater (on a rare cold day), cardboard boxes to cover myself with at night, magazines to read, tape cassettes, an earring, a shopping cart, and even a friendly cocker spaniel. All free. I did see plenty of examples of a barter economy at work, but what I have included here were offered as gifts.

Along with food, clothing, and gadgets, information was also shared among the very poor people I met, but it was only slightly more reliable than that given me by city employees. I was again misdirected to the unemployment office. I was directed to a shelter that proved to be there, and to a goodwill center where used clothing was available. By now I knew the location of certain services. One afternoon on the oceanfront palisades, several men and two women asked me where the nearest soup kitchen was, which I was able to tell them. But a woman in a tattered babushka, watching me give directions to the soup kitchen, gave me the name of a restaurant where she said they passed out free food at closing time, and I was almost arrested when I showed up there. Two drifters told me about an abandoned bathhouse at a Venice beach where I could sleep. I went there the following evening, but it had been boarded up. Perhaps in both cases the information had once been accurate but had become out of date. I was given three wrong addresses for welfare.

But the poor were kind. In the equipoise of dispossession, the people I was looking for, and at, seemed generally glad to have the unaccustomed attention I gave them. This was evident whether I stopped shaving and had a hole in my shirt or was dressed in casual middle-class clothing. Whenever I was able to have a full conversation, I returned to my theme of work among the very poor.

A man and woman I met on the palisades were spending the night there because they mistrusted shelters so much they refused to go to one. The man, 44, had done plumbing and maintenance at nursing homes until he was laid off 10 months earlier. He said he had worked steadily for six years before that, living in an apartment in Venice.

The woman he was with, 40, had worked at a secretary in Washington, D.C., at various government agencies about which she could recount an impressive number of details. She also knew several computer languages. When she was laid off she suffered a breakdown during which she lost her children to a sister-in-law, and now, with her relatives in the East, she felt she had nowhere to turn. The man she was with was white, she was black, and if they could not be said to be living together because they had nowhere to live, they were at least being homeless together. But they were not expecting to survive their hard times. "I have no hopes," she said. "I've given up looking for work after a year and a half of turndowns. I hang with him because he's no druggie, but I haven't any idea what will happen to me." The man was just as indefinite and as futureless. "Where will I be in five years? I'll probably be dead."

Underclass purists would not accept many of the individuals I saw in Santa Monica as true members of the underclass. They are socially and economically immobile—wherever they go they're at the bottom—but not geographically confined. Indeed, they are nomads compared to the locked-in residents of the big Eastern ghettos. They are not from families with no links to the working and middle classes, nor have their grandparents and parents necessarily been as poor as they are. But they are no less stuck, no less mired in poverty and misery, than the urban minority poor. They are without resources for making their lives better, and their experiences with teenage pregnancy, drug addiction, dropping out of school, and petty crime are strikingly similar to those of the ghetto underclass. They are untrained for the kinds of jobs that are available, and they are without prospects.

At the church shelter in Hollywood where I had met the married teenagers Justin and Bryna, men and women in their prime were not doing anything. I felt surrounded by people who were waiting, engines idling, for something to happen. Many of them were migrants to California from the Midwest and East. But when they bestir themselves these days, their movements are coastal along a north-south salient, as if the Pacific Ocean were a magnet whose field allowed its filings only latitudinal shifts in location. They will shuffle up and down the coast between Seattle and San Diego, but wherever they go they are nobody. Perhaps that is a key to the underclass; it is so hard to identify because those who are in it can have very little identity, scant presence, in a society that defines its units economically. Nobody means no body.

A former editor of his college newspaper in Georgia, his intelligence intact but flickering, washed up in the Hollywood shelter the way a piece of driftwood is deposited on the sand by a wave. Barely remembering some of the years between college and his arrival in the shelter, he promised anyone who would listen that he was trying to win back his old self. As one might hope to regain a lost love, I thought. He admitted he had been turned down for so many jobs his spirit was already broken at age 27. "I know I look 42"—and he did—"but that's what the streets do to you. Along with drink. Along with drugs." He'd been clean, he said, for three months, and an attendant in the shelter confirmed this. Still, he could find no steady work. He had picked up cans and bottles for their deposit value, and he had found day jobs through the downtown Los Angeles slave markets, as the lowest-scale employment agencies are known. "Nothing out here lasts, though, you know that?" he said. "Guy tells me he'll have something steady for me next week. Next week comes, he tells me, 'That was then, this is now, get lost.' I already am lost. I don't need him to tell me that."

Cots were set up in neat rows around the church basement, which is spacious enough for a basketball court. Two men were being celebrated by the others; one had just been hired to clean out tour buses, the other had reclaimed his old job in a meat-packing plant. But neither would make enough to move into a home of his own. Neither knew of a house or an apartment he could afford, even with a new job, even though both were willing to have roommates. Moving from the nonworking to the working poor, they would remain homeless, at least in the near future. Homeless did not necessarily mean hopeless. Through his new job, each thought he could find someone with a place to stay.

A bald man with a well-tended mustache sat on a nearby cot. Originally a Midwesterner, he was called Leemy (pronounced lee-me) from his habit of telling others to leave him alone. His father had deserted the family during the Depression, shortly after Leemy was born. His mother worked three jobs, he said, and the third one was hustling. He had worked his way out from Omaha 20 years ago, a short-order cook in roadhouses. Zig-zagging west, he had fathered children along the way—in Wichita, Denver, Salt Lake City, Portland, Seattle—a spermic Johnny Appleseed. He had no remorse for not staying near his children. "The girls wanted them," Leemy said, stroking his mustache. "I was no different than a stud bull. Did my job and moved on."

In Los Angeles Leemy became an assistant chef in restaurants not exactly at the top of the food chain but well up from roadhouses. "I drank, too, the ruin of me," he said. "But I've been dry a year and a month. I'm out looking for a stove to stand over most days now. I'll work again, I know it, I just haven't found a spot yet. I heard of a fancy joint on Melrose just starting up. Maybe I can still do my Maryland crabmeat cakes. Saffron's my secret. Wait till they get a load of my lamb chops smothered in parsley butter. Hint of tarragon." So said Johnny Peopleseed, aka Leemy, caring far more, and knowing more, about his recipes than his children, valued only for his apparently faded skills, valuing himself as he was valued, bequeathing what he had inherited. From a couple of cots away a snore arose as clearly as if taps were being sounded. Tugging his mustache, Leemy bedded down along with the others in the church basement, surrounded yet thoroughly alone.

Leaving the Hollywood shelter I had a sense the country had been leveled as far as the underclass is concerned. The sectional differences that airports, malls, and mass communications tend to obliterate were also obliterated by extreme poverty. Down was the only direction, out was the only fixed position. What "Hollywood" meant in faraway schoolyards or in supermarkets or on rap records mattered little here, where "Hollywood" meant just another place to flop. Work for the poorest poor had become as hard to find in Los

Angeles, a beacon of opportunity for most of the century, as in the supposedly wornout, rusty places people were escaping from when they migrated west.

When I returned to San Antonio, I saw the effects of cultural dislocation on underclass work. In Mexico the peasant families had been poor, but an individual's labor had a secure place within an overall feudal structure. The work was raising crops and children; each could be done with skill and pride. In the United States the harsh old rules of a landed oligarchy no longer applied, but the freedom to be anything went hand in hand with the ability to do nothing the new society valued very highly. When the low-paying, unskilled jobs were lost to automation, many Mexican-Americans, particularly the men, were left without economic legs to stand on.

Although the residents of the Alazan Apache Courts in San Antonio at least had housing, their standing in the labor market was as tenuous as what I had found at the Hollywood shelter. Alazan Apache reality didn't leave room for the California dreams I was still able to hear occasionally on the West Coast. A common theme was bluntly expressed by a Mexican-American who is also a third-generation Texan. His last job, janitor in a bowling alley, had ended a year and a half before I met him. "I guess I've lost hope," he said with finality. "You lose that, you can't find it again." He drew no welfare of his own, sharing the Social Security and disability checks of a blind man he took care of.

Other Alazan Apache residents had been laid off from a stagnant construction industry, lost jobs in shut-down oilfields, failed to make the cut when companies they worked for tightened their belts. Like the former bowling alley janitor, they expressed less anger than discouragement. They told me they simply didn't know what to do anymore.

Like anyone who has lived or worked with them, I knew that among the Mexican-American poor the Catholic Church remains a central authority. Yet the underclass at the bottom of the poverty scale, though reached—or, in the altruists' idiom, "outreached"— by numerous Church missions, were not telling me they looked to their religion as a source of security. Was the Church as impotent as the government in dealing with the persistently poor? After listening to some of the poorest people of San Antonio describe the blind alleys of their lives, I made a date to see an old friend, Father Ralph Ruiz, whom I had worked with over 20 years earlier investigating hunger and poverty. While the Church has other goals besides combating poverty, as does the government, numerous Catholic reformers in the mold of Dorothy Day and Michael Harrington devoted most of their lives to obeying the scriptural injunction to help the helpless. I was curious as to how Father Ruiz's idealism had weathered the decades.

When I knew Father Ruiz in the '60s, almost all of his considerable energies went toward helping the very poor. As far as I could see then, he never rested. In the '90s, still a humanitarian, his certainties have vanished, both theologically and sociologically. He is no longer Father but Mr., having given up his priesthood principally in frustration with what he experienced as a status-quo hierarchy. Ralph Ruiz is now married with three children, and, though still a Catholic, he organizes service missions for the Lutherans. He is stocky and gray as once he was stocky and black-haired, he is measured where once he was angry, and he is comfortable where once he was agitated—and, indeed, an agitator. Still full of the desire to do good work toward the elimination of poverty, my old friend was no longer nearly as confident of the prospects for social ascent among the poor as he once had been.

"The cycles of inheritance are what's so disturbing," Ralph Ruiz told me. "Is the Bible right—'the poor are always with you'—I don't know." I asked him to think about the changes he has witnessed. "We seem to have replaced the culture of poverty with the culture of dependence," he said. "And it's more violent. There may be less hunger now in San Antonio, but there are more drugs and more violence. The Mexicano has learned to use guns when he always used to use knives, so the violence is more lethal. They used to be cut, now they end up dead."

He had spent decades trying to help the poor help themselves. He had made notable efforts to help the society above the poor awaken to the problem at its feet. Yet he was not the idealistic activist I had once known. Was it wisdom he had achieved or burnout he had suffered?

It was with something approaching despair that Ralph Ruiz looked at me and answered my question by evaluating the successor problems to the ones we had evaluated together in the '60s. "What I know is I walk through the projects today, and I see the people I have always known. I knew their parents, I knew their grandparents, now I know the third generation. They are still there. What has happened is they have left their shacks and are now in public housing, but it's the same people I've known for 25 years, still there, still very poor, still without a path upwards that they know how to follow."

Ralph Ruiz, a station on my journey as he had been in the '60s, had reason to be discouraged. The persistently poor of San Antonio were poorer, more persistent, and more numerous than they had been in the '60s. In 1994, according to a Rockefeller Foundation survey, almost 400,000 of the city's residents were poor. Yet part of the '60s war on poverty had been won, even in San Antonio. Poverty programs had skimmed off those who were most reachable, and they had become self-sufficient. The rest sank back, untrained and un-lifted, into a kind of self-replicating and, in view of the numbers of their children, self-multiplying misery. Ralph Ruiz's observations had me floundering, too, as I headed again for Bangor. American society was breeding its underclass as efficiently as a marsh breeds mosquitoes.

In the Bangor soup kitchen before lunch was brought out by volunteers from a local church, it was not ordinary body odor permeating the dining room, neither the kind that comes from physical labor nor the nervous kind that builds up in offices. There was the cloying essence of overripe fruit kept too long in a barrel. As in the homes of the rich, where floral scents mingle with perfume, furniture polish, old leather, and the cleanser that has been used on the Bokhara rugs, it was not clear in the soup kitchen exactly what was the source of which fragrance. Onions, tomatoes, tobacco (though not being smoked or chewed inside the Salvation Army building), apples, beery breath, disinfectant, clothing that had several owners, a cheesy exhaust—all of them could be detected among the gathering. These were the smells of living but not of making a living.

No one there was on any job that day, or on any day I went there. Halftime Henry was a shoemaker who had been laid off four weeks before I first saw him. He didn't talk a great deal, most of his communication coming from his eyes. His eyes were those of a deer or a prisoner about to be shot. With an angry birthmark beside his frightened left eye, Henry looked as if someone or something, destiny itself, had already fired at him. Yet his eyes seemed still to plead, both for escape and approval. Black, slicked-back hair combed into a duck-tail gave Henry the look of a man who had never left the '50s.

Now 48 years old, Henry was once a cheerleader for his high school football team, performing mostly at halftime, an activity that yielded his nickname. He had ditched the nickname for about 20 years until an old classmate came to work at the same shoe factory. After that no one called him anything except Halftime Henry. He lived up to that name, or down to it, leaving the impression of a man whose efforts were not part of anyone's main show, even his own, but rather of a pleasing interval between sessions in which the main business was conducted.

Henry's shoes, which he had made himself, were even shinier than his slick hair. When he wasn't working or at the soup kitchen, he liked to walk back and forth over the oldest of the three bridges that span the Penobscot River connecting Bangor to its sister town, Brewer. He has never been married. "Never wanted much of anything," Halftime Henry said, eschewing the first-person singular. "Got along with everyone, didn't want to live with anyone." On his professional life, he was equally terse, equally self-effacing. "Sixty dollars a week was what you could get along on when we started. Odd jobs would bring it in. Takes more now, not too much more, but more. Shoemakin's useful." He had lost his mobile home in a fire three months before he lost his job; he then moved into an apartment in Brewer. His misfortunes were piling up. The day before I met him, Halftime Henry had been turned out of his apartment for owing too much back rent, and he was taking temporary refuge at the Bangor shelter.

At a table near the entrance to the soup kitchen, a Social Security field representative named Robert Connor set up shop one day. He had come essentially to solicit business, reaching out to help those who came to shelters and soup kitchens. Specifically, Connor was offering Social Security Disability and Supplemental Security Income. These are forms of public assistance available to those who are physically disabled, mentally deficient, or emotionally disturbed. In the bigger cities I visited, I never saw anyone like Connor, a federal official, trying to give the government's money away to those who qualified for it but might not have known about it or how to go about getting it. Several applicants milled around Connor's table, not a deluge, but Connor told me he felt his presence was helpful, and I thought it was a good sign when the government's representatives asked citizens how they could be of use. Government for the people. I did not think it was a good sign that in the big cities I never saw a Robert Connor.

Bob Roster was one of those who, as he was shortly to make clear, could qualify for aid but who did not approach Robert Connor. Roster was in an argument at his luncheon table. His antagonist was the unruly teenager Bull Penner, whom I'd seen several times at the Salvation Army building. The volunteers at the soup kitchen, often retired women (and a few men) from churches in nearby towns, were infallibly well mannered as well as tolerant, and one of their few rules was that people behave themselves in the dining room. Bob Roster, irritated, finished his meal quickly. Hurrying outside, Roster, the only black man at the soup kitchen, stood toe to toe with Bull Penner, their beards almost touching. They were in a dispute over whether the main course had been chicken or turkey. I thought possibly Bull had been drinking before lunch, and everyone knew Bob Roster was, as a soup kitchen regular named Denver Dave put it, "not exactly playing with a full deck." Brown beard against black beard: Who would win? They were mammoth, creatures of field or forest, strangers in any townscape, each capable of Bunyanesque feats in the town that prides itself on being Paul Bunyan's roost. In a moment they would be like bears fighting over the leavings in an abandoned campground, or they could be tumbling and playing like cubs. Bull laughed first. "Ha ha, just pullin' your chain, Bob. It probably was turkey with the drumsticks that size." Bob was never whimsical, but he was glad not to fight. "We have set an example in problem resolution for the peoples of the universe. Message received, you may turn off your transponder. Thank you, Bull."

Bob Roster spent his afternoons at the public library. This made sense with the cold weather coming on, but he was also doing research that was very important to him. "I've worked most recently as a welder," he told me, "and before that as a sign painter. The money was extraordinary as a welder, minimal when I painted signs. It all culminated in the Northeast downturn of the early '90s. After that, a brief excursion, shall we say holiday, in a mental health facility."

Words such as "minimal" and "culminated," even if used a little differently from the way they would be used by most people, came easily to Bob Roster. In letting me know he was out of work, he also wanted me to know he read a lot. Soft-spoken as well as polysyllabic, he had stepped away from his usual character in his brief confrontation with Bull Penner. When I asked if he received welfare or unemployment checks, he grew even quieter. "Public help is demeaning," he said, "and it's more trouble than it's worth." I told Bob Roster that a Social Security representative had been at the soup kitchen offering to help applicants receive assistance for various forms of disability. "Once they enlist you on their rolls, they plant the transponder on you," he answered. "You're in their toils forever, and your confidential file enlarges every day."

Bob asked me what kind of work I do. "Writing? I hadn't realized things had gotten that bad," he said gently, looking around the soup kitchen vicinity, "but I guess times must be tough all over."

Between his lunch at the Salvation Army, which closes at 1:15 after being open for an hour and a half, and his lodging at the Bangor shelter, which opens at 6:00 P.M., Bob Roster went to the library. In his fashion, he was working there. He drew me aside to divulge the nature of his research. "My present studies involve the possible linkage between the FBI, the CIA, and assorted other federal agencies who are planting electromagnetic devices among the populace for purposes unknown and only dreamt of by angels or devils, I'm not yet sure which." Did racial prejudice make Bob Roster suspicious of unseen forces? "Prejudice would be one source, yes, but only one. Nobody, white or black, can elude the radiation now coursing among us."

Emotionally disturbed members of the underclass, such as Bob Roster, present an entire subcategory of persistently poor, with problems of their own in addition to the blight of poverty. I have noticed a number of damaged people around the country, mostly out of work. They have a schedule, a routine, a strategy for surviving, but this does not include going to a job or looking for one. They might, however, make a practical decision to do so if it were rewarding. Some I spoke to—emotionally disturbed or mildly retarded— appear to be saying, one way or another, the following: I bounce around here and there to get by on my street knowledge, but I can't trade what I know for dollars on any regular basis. Specialists familiar with the emotional problems of the homeless have suggested sheltered workshops where mildly disturbed people could find regular employment. A few of these workshops exist but only on an experimental basis. The great majority of this subcategory, whose members range from the disturbed to the retarded, do very little work. They are treated as social castoffs, unhappily saddled with a sense of uselessness.

Every economic class has its round pegs for round holes, those who fit perfectly and wouldn't want to be anywhere else. The most consistently employed worker at the Bangor soup kitchen was Denver Dave. He is over six feet tall, beginning to have a slightly round, weathered face, and he enjoys making friends. Like approximately one-third of the men I met at the soup kitchen, Dave said he doesn't drink. Unlike a number of the others, he feels no sense of social deprivation at not having a steady job or permanent home. He would categorically reject any description of himself that included the word "loser." Smiling most of the time, his easy sociability made him popular with almost everyone he came in contact with at the soup kitchen and the downtown shelter.

Dave was brought up in an orphanage outside Denver that was run by the Capuchins. He remembered the friars raising him in a strict but fair manner. He played first base at their high school. "I was scouted, too," he recalled with some pride, "had a chance to start in the high minors, but I knew even then I didn't belong on a team of any kind, so I just took off."

Without parents or any family he knew of, Dave hit the open road and has pretty much stayed there. He rides a patched-up Honda motorcycle all over the country and finds work almost whenever he needs it. He'll pick oranges or blueberries, depending on what state or season he is in, clean yards, haul junk, or drive a delivery truck as long as he doesn't have to promise anyone he'll be doing the same thing next month. His belongings all fit on the Honda, and he has no interest in collecting what won't fit. "Just tie you down, possessions, that's all they do."

Dave had a regular job at the age of 24, driving an interstate truck route. He saw an older driver die at the wheel from a heart attack one day as they pulled into a truck stop outside Louisville. "That was it for me," he remembered. "Fella was 60, and I looked at him and thought, 'Sorry, old buddy, but better you than me.' I learned my lesson—that wasn't about to be how I ended up. I said no more sitting in the same driver's seat and sleeping up behind it, no more eyes pasted to the double yellow in front of me, no more harness of any kind for me, so goodbye. That was my last regular job."

Ten years later, at 34, Dave basically migrates for a living. "Hell, no!" he boomed when I asked if he gets public assistance. "Why not? PRIDE! That's why." Plus, he didn't add, he isn't the type to stay in one place long enough to qualify. Besides his Honda, Dave owns three pairs of dungarees, seven t-shirts, two coats, two sweaters, three workshirts, and a bedroll. Once, a few years ago, Dave had a home, an apartment in Tallahassee. "Trouble was, things got so I was thinking about how I needed some drapes and the roof leaked, so I had to get rid of it before it became a total burden."

Dave planned on wintering in Savannah and Galveston. "I have some friends both places, and the missions are hospitable. Both places I can get work." He jumped on his Honda after lunch and was preparing to cycle down the road that runs alongside the Penobscot River, returning to Bangor to use the downtown shelter in the evening. "Nice day for a jaunt, isn't it?" Dave said. "You know, if freedom is happiness, I've got both." Off Dave went in a roar from the Honda's pipes. He is hardly underclass in the strict sense William Julius Wilson uses the term. Dave is geographically mobile and works when he wants, not pinned down in a dead-end ghetto. He has a checkerboard past and an uncertain future economically as well as socially. It is almost impossible to mention Denver Dave and the word "poor" in the same sentence, but that is, of course, the way statisticians rank him. Most of his companions are destitute or at least well outside the boundaries of making a living. The question is, How long can anyone keep up a life like Denver Dave's? What happens when he and his Honda get creaky? The older versions of Dave whom I met—visions, really, of Dave in 20 years—predict his place among the persistently poor.

But Denver Dave is a rarity. When the New England winter struck, he was long gone. The people who lined up in Bangor at the Salvation Army's doorstep tended to be hard-core unemployed. A social worker acquainted with the soup kitchen estimated that about half of the regulars had emotional problems that kept them out of the conventional workforce. Beginning almost a generation ago, advances in medication allowed a high percentage of the patients of crowded mental hospitals to be released into the general population. No advance, of course, has provided these former mental patients with the alarm clock that will remind them to take their medicine every day. Reductions in mental health budgets have also *forced* them out of the hospitals in the past decade.

Liberals and conservatives collaborated to deinstitutionalize and, in a sense, dispossess these marginally functioning adults. The liberals wanted to free them from physical restraints by using the new chemical mood stabilizers. The conservatives wanted to save money by getting them off the state's hands. Often, former mental patients return to families with few resources and marginal stability of their own. The promised community mental health centers never bloomed in most communities. At the same time, cuts of affordable housing have prevented these former patients from obtaining available homes because the homes are not available. The homeless are not all emotionally disturbed; nor, manifestly, are the disturbed all homeless. The correlation, however, is obvious. A formula for increasing the visible underclass emerges: thorazine + decaying asylums − mental health funds = walking wounded in the street.

Emotional problems merge seamlessly with drug habits in disabling a number of those I met among the persistently poor. At 40, Ron Gormley is an ex-hippie who believes he never came down from an accidental PCP trip in 1979. "I was a computer technician married to a nice Jewish girl from Philadelphia," he said, "when someone stuck the PCP in my coffee. After that it was skid row for a decade—Nashville, LA, D.C., lot of places, two years flat on my back in Augusta, Maine." He wore a big fur hat against the February freeze; his red beard was streaked with frost. "I'm getting welfare now until I can find menial work. Just menial, I'll never do computers again. You're writing a book? I wrote my own vision of the future and printed 1,000 copies. I got Stephen King's endorsement. Say, Buddy, who's your publisher?"

Ron Gormley rambled on. The author Stephen King, who lives in Bangor, is a local folk hero. Many drifters claim either to have King's endorsement for a book or else that King has plagiarized their work. One such drifter broke into King's house and scared his wife, who was home alone at the time. After he was captured in the attic, the intruder excused himself by asserting that King terrified millions whereas he had frightened only one person.

An endearing quality of gentle, self-deprecating humor is shared by many of the street people among the underclass. Occasionally, they scare others but are usually harmless. Liking these people as I did, I was feeling a conflict between my perception of their deprivation and their eccentricities. The latter had a charm that was sneaking up on me as I continued my journey among the underclass. The former remained as appalling to me as it was painful to them.

Unlike Ron Gormley, Bruce Hall and his wife Elsie do have their own apartment, but he was laid off from his grave-digging job in November and it would not resume until April. "The deceased," he said decorously, "are placed in a tomb to wait for spring burial when the ground thaws." Paid off the books, Bruce Hall could not qualify for unemployment benefits. He and his wife, both in their 40s, depend on local charity. A half-brother of Elsie Hall's occasionally sends them a small check from Arizona, and the couple spend many of their days pacing up and down the sidewalks of Bangor until the grave-digging season begins again. "We always wanted children and never could have them," Bruce Hall said. "If I can't provide any better than this, I guess those unborn babies are lucky."

Adriana Saint Duclos Mathere, whose observation on the wants of the poor began this chapter, had not worked steadily all winter since her blueberry packing job ended in the fall. She found occasional temporary work as a cook's assistant in cheap restaurants, and she recalls having had the distinction of leading a sitdown strike among the disenfranchised workers at a local fair. "The wackos and misfits who work these fairs a week at a time are people living in soul-destroying poverty," she told me one day after lunch at the soup kitchen. "The management of the fair was stiffing the poorest workers out of several thousand dollars of back wages. I became their Norma Rae, stood up to management, and threatened to shut down the fair on their biggest day, Saturday. By God, we got the money."

Adriana smiled her enigmatic smile, which contended with a message of loneliness from her eyes. She is a perfect example of someone I found quite frequently among the underclass. She is highly intelligent but has problems of focus and stability. At times these problems are difficult to discern and she is apparently normal; at other times she is visibly disoriented. Her existence answers a rhetorical question I had posed early in my research: Do the under-class suffer from a lack of innate skill and intelligence? No, most of them don't, but in addition to lacking saleable training, they are often undone by stress and complexity.

Whenever I saw Adriana, her feelings were at a flashpoint in more than one direction. If she was sad she was also serene. If she laughed she was also ready with tears. "Oh, but the management of that county fair hated me," Adriana went on. "They swore I'd never have a job there again. But I did them a favor. I made the workers stay in line. Do you have any idea how hard it is to keep a dozen of these drunks sober for a whole weekend during the fair?"

I have seen Adriana a number of times. One day some of the former workers from the fair confirmed her story by bringing her free clothes that had been donated in a dumpster outside the Salvation Army building. They needed the clothes themselves and could have kept them, but they made sure Adriana had the best-looking sweater and topcoat. "Thanks for gettin' us our pay, good lady," one of them said. Another day I took her to a real restaurant for lunch, but she ordered only coffee. Her appetite hasn't been very good lately, she said. She is always polite and articulate, both about herself and others, and she is usually melancholy and somewhat apprehensive. Her two young children, one of them sickly, are with their father, from whom she is divorced. She misses them with a tangible agony, living for the occasional weekend when she can visit them.

Recalling her childhood with an alcoholic father, Adriana said her mother could never serve peas for dinner because her father's hand shook so much he couldn't get the peas from his plate to his mouth on a fork. Adriana looks like a French Canadian Gilda Radner— flirting eyes under heavy lids, a ready smile, sadness beneath the smile. She is pretty the way Gilda Radner was and also unpretty like her. "I've done social mobility in reverse," she said, chuckling at herself. "Gone from middle-class housewife to pauper, and now I'm trying to bounce back up into the working poor. I need a job that lasts longer than three weeks, but I need to get *me* into a position where I can last in a regular job. I think I've solved most of what was holding me back." Vague as she left the details of what held her back, she was clearly a suffering woman whose troubles had not permitted her full functioning up to the level of her considerable intelligence. She could work hard and well at a variety of tasks; she could also unravel in a manner that would exclude a regular job. "When you know what you're aiming for," she said, "it's so much easier to get it. But when the world forgets you, and it does try to forget the poor, it also forgets to leave you space where you can go after what you're aiming for."

Reflecting on what exactly it is that causes the underclass so much trouble with work, I often recalled the situation of Kelso Dana, Jr. I met him again, the teenager with the torturing father and slightly bluish teeth, at the Bangor shelter when I arrived one winter evening. Like most members of the underclass I met, he was no welfare cheat and neither was he consistently employed. Indeed, like so many of the persistently poor I saw all around the country, he was not receiving the full benefits various laws entitle him to. This shows how massive the welfare problem really is; even those who haven't worked in years, perhaps have never worked, are very hard to classify as cheats. Very few can simply be kicked off the rolls. They don't work because they can't. They can't find work and can't do it if they do find it. No single catchall program is ever going to scoop them all up and convert them into employable citizens. They have a variety of problems that require, if the national will were there, a variety of solutions.

Kelso was playing checkers in the shelter with Halftime Henry. Though furnished simply, the Bangor shelter is a homey place next to a shop that sells Christmas decorations all year long. It had been six months since I'd seen Kelso. His teeth were no longer blue. They were also no longer his own, as I was about to learn, and he was no longer a teenager either. His girlfriend Polly was pregnant, but she was not at the shelter because she stays with a relative. Kelso was proud of Polly's pregnancy, and somehow he cadged enough money that afternoon to buy her roses.

All of Kelso's teeth had recently been pulled. What happened was that at some point in his passage to maturity, at some point when his father was no longer able to get at him, Kelso replaced his father as his own principal torturer. He would swallow bleach sometimes, other times get into fights with several people at once, when he knew he'd be severely beaten. He would also swallow other household cleansers as well as plastic and even glass. Finally, his teeth rotted beyond even root canal reclamation. Kelso had turned 20 and now had a full set of false teeth. His features were still those of a Norse god, but when he took out his dentures his face shriveled toward his mouth like that of a prematurely old man. He tussled playfully at the shelter with a friend who was an unemployed ditch digger, then he settled down to tell me about his own work.

With all the pain and fury in his background, Kelso has tried to become a productive member of the labor force. He has worked as a janitor in three schools, mopped the floors of the Bangor City Hall, cleaned up a local ice rink after hockey games and the concert hall after the musicians and audience have left. When he hit the road, Kelso was a machine operator in the South and later ran a five-inch blade saw in a lumber mill. "You think I'm 20, and *I* think I'm 20," he said, "but I'm 100 years old on the street." What he lacked was training in a specific skill that would keep him employed and the emotional stability that would permit job regularity. He believed both these were within reach. He told me he had become much calmer than he was a few months earlier, and he was determined to get back in the workforce. "After all, I've always paid my way."

Sometimes even after he is checked in for the night Kelso has to leave the shelter for a half-hour or so. "I can't stand confinement, you know," he said, referring to his days and nights imprisoned in his father's well. Susan Brainerd, a social worker who has five children of her own, runs the Bangor shelter with the loving patience much of the world associates with Mother Teresa. She allows Kelso the freedom he needs in order to feel comfortable, then reins him in if he disrupts others. "He's someone you treat carefully," Susan Brainerd said to me, "because he's someone who can transcend his background of suffering if he gets the chance. You want to give him the chance."

Returning from a short walk, Kelso borrowed loose tobacco from his friend Halftime Henry and rolled himself a cigarette for the next time he went outside. "Day labor is my future for now," Kelso said. "After that, we'll see." He went to Susan Brainerd's office to borrow something to read, returning with a volume of Freud and a mystery. As I was leaving the shelter, he sank into an easy chair in the common room. Kelso read Freud. He looked up at me. "This time next year, you see, I'm going to be a father."

6

Parents

Building the New Generation

If the persistently poor cannot get and keep jobs, there must be a reason. After we finish blaming an inadequate school system, an incompetent welfare bureaucracy, advances in technology that move meaningful work out of their reach, we still have not accounted for the permanence of poverty among the underclass. We have to look at underclass parents. The central reason for an underclass child growing into what social psychologists call dysfunctional maturity is the family that produces the child. The replication of the underclass generation after generation relies, unsurprisingly, on the replication of underclass parents.

In the families of the poor, 66 percent of children under the age of six have unmarried mothers. When we consider the very poorest poor—the underclass—this figure takes flight to over 80 percent. But in the noisy debate over "family breakdown," we miss a point. For most underclass parents and their children, there never was a conventional family to do any breaking down. The structure of an underclass family is vertical, usually from grandmother to mother to child, not horizontal with a bond between a mother and father forming the basis for the next generation. The emotional consequences of either a vertical or a horizontal structure are not so inherently crippling or nurturing as they are self-sustaining. We tend to become the parents we had unless there is a very good reason to do otherwise.

The central truth about any parent in the underclass is that an underclass parent is a parent. Everything else follows. This echoes Adriana Saint Duclos Mathere's remark to me that the poor want what everyone else wants, which turns over to mean that they also do not want what everyone else doesn't want. Mathere herself, working and not working in the countryside around Bangor, smiling and tearful in her struggles, is a parent grieving over children who no longer live with her.

In contemplating our own lives, we can readily acknowledge that we would be devastated if we were unable to take care of our children—to feed, clothe, and shelter them properly. If we lost them to the streets or to a state agency that was somehow able to remove them from our keep, we might become violent, depressed, possibly paralyzed by the futility of anything we could do to get them back. If we were trying to survive in a municipal ghetto, we would be surrounded by drugs and disease as well as the threat and actuality of violence. We would regard a phrase like "self-esteem" as a mean joke. Lurching among depression, resolve, and apathy, we might hunker down the way Ronnielee Divine did in Oakland and eventually regain custody of our children. We might be grimly determined, like Dinah Lou Freeman with her three sons in the Chicago projects, to somehow burst our children out of the chains we ourselves are bound by. We might also collapse, especially if we had too many other problems to count.

But when we consider these catastrophes among a generic under-class—losing children to the streets or to an arm of the state—it is as though they were being visited on another species of life altogether, one that is not quite human with not quite human feelings. Does the lack of money equal an unhumanness in which we would lose not only our ability to eat and sleep comfortably but also our ability to feel pain? If we were born into the underclass as Dinah Lou Freeman was, or plummeted there as Adriana Saint Duclos Mathere did, would we also be without the eyesight to visualize a better condition? This is unlikely when you recall how many times an hour television thrusts dazzling cars, vintage wines, gleaming jewelry, barbecuing steaks, elegant homes, pricey fur coats in front of all of us, underclass as well as upper classes. Yet somehow those of us who enjoy balmy days tend to behave as if people who encounter stormy weather don't know the difference between rain and a rainbow.

The underclass does not always help the rest of us here. Their own behavior at times makes it easier for us to turn away. Some of the persistently poor act as though parenthood were too much of a burden to bear or simply something they want nothing to do with. (Members of the upper classes may act the same way, but they are able to disguise their apathy and outright antipathy, from strangers if not from their children, with stratagems the underclass cannot afford.) It is easy to lose sympathy with this kind of parent. The hours and days I enjoyed least in my travels were spent with individuals who had produced other individuals and then refused to nurture them. It was always, of course, more complicated than my first impression.

From what I was able to see and know of him, when Hector Zacario thinks about who he is and where he is, he tries hard not to. He lives, if that is the right word, in and out of the decaying Alazan Apache Courts in San Antonio. Hector Zacario presents an easily recognizable figure in American history and literature: the wastrel who contributes almost nothing to his children yet wants a piece of whatever crumbs may fall their way. If he sees his children going to school, he is jealous they may wind up smarter than he is. He hits them when he's sober, threatens them with a knife when he's drunk. He's a one-man horror show, yet he cannot stay away from his kids, cannot hide his need for them, cannot simply abandon them even when his selfish schemes for exploiting them are repeatedly foiled. We all know him from America's favorite coming of age story. He is Huckleberry Finn's father.

Like old Pap Finn, Hector Zacario is shunned even by the poor.

Like Pap Finn, he tries to get his children's food and what little money they have. He has been run out of Alazan Apache, and he stays away for a while, but he always manages to slink back, stay at a relative's apartment, sponge off the aunt who is bringing up his children after the death of their mother. A tall, bent man with hair still black at 50, he has a torn ear from one of his inevitable brawls, and he limps from the time a car hit him as he lay drunk on a curb. Hector Zacario has tried to sue the man who hit him with the car, a man who was also drunk, but he failed even at that. He draws no welfare, unable to show up for appointments on any regular basis. When he works he repairs motorcycles for neighborhood teenagers who are a little better off than he is, and he also collects bottles and cans for their redemption value.

"You can call me the great redeemer," Hector Zacario said to me when I asked him how he kept going when he worked so little and drank so much. "I pick up everything that holds the stingo people get drunk on, also I pick up the empty Cokes and Pepsis, I redeem the cans and bottles for cash, and pretty soon I can get drunk again myself." We were standing outside an open area where a few boys, including his son, were playing soccer. I asked him how he felt about his children, a boy of 11 and a girl of nine. He swayed a little, not really drunk yet—it was only 11:00 in the morning—and steadied himself against a stair railing. "You know, I feel like I gave them the best years of my life and now I want something back. Flesh of my flesh, I own them until they're 18, don't I? Doesn't a man have a right to his own kids if he don't have nothing else? If this is a free country, these kids have to do what I say until they got their own power, no?"

I already had heard from his sister-in-law, the children's aunt, that Hector Zacario had hardly given the best years of his life, if there were any best years, to either his children or his late wife. Yet here he was, just like Pap Finn, figuring he owned his children. He had tried to get them to quit school and work the streets as beggars so he wouldn't have to pick up cans and bottles anymore. There was not much point in judging Hector Zacario, so I tried to find out how he became who he was.

"Oh, I'm from right here, Alazan Apache," he said, scratching his torn ear. "My family came to San Antone maybe 40 years ago, not from Mexico, from over in Corpus. I bet we've been Americans longer than you, Mr. Anglo. Corpus Christi couldn't hold us so we came over here, moved to Alazan Apache maybe one of the first families back in the '50s. First family in the project. But I was born drunk, what can I tell you? I try to reform. I get sober sometimes for months, I'll get me a little job, straight as an arrow, I'll do some brass plating, some carpentry. Stay off the wine and whisky, maybe just a beer or two after work."

Shakily, holding onto the stair railing, Hector Zacario wobbled up to the top step. I thought he was going to try to get into the apartment the steps mounted to, but he only wanted to use the stoop to place himself above me, or for a view of the project, or for his pulpit. He swept his bloodshot eyes over the other pocked stoops and ruined doorways, the scarred walls and shattered windows of Alazan.

"I'll head out for Laredo if I hear of some construction this side of the border," he said, laying claim to more initiative than I'd been told he normally exhibited, "and I'll pretend to be a wetback and work for next to nothing, just any kind of work. Store me a few pennies. But the place here it draws me back, my kids, I like to see them grow, and it's the place I've always known. I might go to sleep in Laredo, but I wake me up at Alazan Apache. Every time. Happens every time." He said this as if he were on some long Texas snake of a train traveling the same track endlessly. Whatever other stops the train made, always Hector Zacario would awaken at the Alazan Apache terminus. It was his destiny.

He took an unsteady stride down the steps toward me. Unsure if he meant to swing at me or was about to fall down, I took a step backward. He swayed, and became aware he was swaying. "I guess I got me half a bag on right now, don't I?" He apparently had stepped forward only to emphasize what he wanted to say.

"In this society you don't go nowhere no more. Not if you're me. I see Anglos way up there, I see the Chinese zooming, I even see black guys pushing up, the lazy bastards. Country's going in the shitcan. Some of the Latinos move ahead, not in this neighborhood. When you're on the bottom, man, you stay there, flat down in Alazan Apache."

He was intriguing; Hector Zacario saddened me and angered me too. A drunken, racist, abusive bully, a hypocrite where his neglected offspring were concerned, just like Pap Finn. The aunt bringing up his son and daughter had seven children of her own, and the Zacario children got the leavings in her cramped apartment, at her crowded table. No one was really looking out for them, and it did not take a prophet to see in Hector's son and daughter a new underclass generation. It was clear Hector thought he cared about his children. Surely they were part of the reason he always returned to Alazan Apache. He tried to make money off them, yet he also wanted to be around them. Like Pap Finn, there was something about his progeny that drew him back. Like Pap Finn, he was doing nothing that would bring any benefit to his children. Few obstacles were being placed in the children's path, either by their family or by society, that could prevent their becoming versions of their father. They would wake up where he woke up.

Most of us pride ourselves on being the opposite of Hector Zacario. How we preen over our abilities as parents! We are always building the future in America, and the future begins with our kids. But what if the kids have no future? Is that what Hector Zacario instinctively knows? Underclass parents who care about their children lack resources to give them something better than the falling down carcass of Alazan Apache. Perhaps our claims for ourselves as parents involve less the instinct for nurturing we would like to feel we have and more a kind of class pride that we will at least keep our children out of the gutter that awaits the dispossessed child of disenfranchised parents. Our class pride distances us from any emotional identification with the persistently poor, who become the bedraggled and reeking "other" that can be no part of us. We are safe from them, saved from being them. As long as we don't stray near them, they cannot touch us in either sense of the word.

I myself was as alienated from the Hector Zacarios and Dinah Lou Freemans—the one a member of the "undeserving" poor, the other a sure bet for middle-class (or, as a social worker put it, "meddle-class") sympathies—as if they had been fossils from an ice age cave. But then I met them. Knowing underclass parents as I have come to know them makes me embarrassed about my own vanity as a father. Perhaps it is a sham, my exalted view of myself as a parent, especially my pride in my own parental performance, which I of course don't think of as a performance at all but as an expression of my deepest urges. I have mentioned earlier that I behave more consistently as a father than I do in any other relationship. How touching. Perhaps I only want to see myself reflected, recollected, reproduced, so I'll still be here when I'm not here.

Is there something smug, self-congratulatory, in my inclusion of this speculation here? Or am I putting myself, my precious fatherhood, on the line, inducing you to say, He thinks he's a good father, but maybe all this clucking over his brood is stifling to them. Maybe they loathe him, secretly, can't wait to slip out of his narcissistic grasp, can't wait for him to exit the space they occupy.

Such thoughts are prompted by my observations among underclass parents. As Adriana Saint Duclos Mathere might say, they don't feel different from other parents. Even Hector Zacario, who can be found in any class, homes back to his children, and because his schemes to indenture them invariably come to nothing, I can only conclude he must be drawn by the unbreakable pull of mutual belonging. Underclass parents assuredly cherish their children; they want to protect, provide, pass along values. What's different about them is the ability to protect and provide the way middle-class parents do. Among the underclass discouragement has led to denial, to lowered—vastly lowered—expectations. For mothers, this often means repeating the behavior and results of the previous generation. What is known as tradition in other classes becomes self-replicating misery among the extreme poor.

Where underclass fathers are concerned, discouragement and humiliation have led often to abandonment, which only increases the

misery of the women and children left behind. Because they can't
protect, provide, set examples, play, discipline, and share in the ways
our society promotes and everywhere approves, fathers sometimes
simply opt out. The rules relating to public relief have made
abandonment a necessity, even a sign of fiscal responsibility, among
underclass fathers. The formula is deadly. Aid to families with
dependent children is itself dependent on a family's being broken in
one way or another. AFDC is not granted to a two-parent household
where the father is able to work. With a low income that barely puts
his household over the AFDC limit, a working father can lose his
family's entire monthly relief check. It is a federal requirement that a
two-parent family have a history of work in order to qualify for
AFDC. There is no such requirement in a single-parent household. If
fathers are present and not disabled, their families often cannot get
help; if they are fled, deadbeat, welfare is at least a possibility.

   Bad parenting, it seems fair to say, is built in, is a given, when we
consider the underclass. Good parenting is a courageous, almost
eccentric, exception. The links between coming from a dysfunctional
family and falling into the trapped underclass, or continuing there,
are so strong they are visible in the homes, the shelters, the habits of
the underclass. It will be much easier for Kelso Dana to reproduce his
deprived Maine family, as abusive as it was, than to break the
generational mold and become a new kind of father.

   What seemed to be a carefree, harmless existence when I met
Denver Dave—a man who sped around the country on his Honda
chasing good climates and temporary work—was transformed into
pain when he considered whom he had left behind. The pain was
both caused and felt by him. The only part of his experience the
otherwise cheerful Denver Dave doesn't like to tell about is his
fatherhood. He was married for a while and had no children, then
had a son by a woman he wasn't married to. "I cared so much for
that little boy, Randy Bob, I guess I've never been as happy as when
I'd give him a bath and read him to sleep," Denver Dave told me over
lunch in the Bangor soup kitchen. "But then I never can stay in one
place. I had a little problem with Randy Bob's mom so I split on

them. When I left Tulsa I planned on coming back in a month. I missed the baby so much I was back in two weeks. His little grin would reel you in from Tibet. But you know, me and my Honda and the road. Another sign of trouble, I was off again. When I was in Tulsa next time, there was another guy. I split for good."

Denver Dave sighed. He seemed to feel in over his head. I found my hostility to deserting fathers melting a little into something approaching pity for Dave. He certainly deserved whatever he got from the woman in Tulsa, but that didn't mean he was ineligible to feel pain. "Whew, don't like recollecting this," he said. "My lady, she went and married the guy and taught Randy Bob to call the new dad 'Dad' and think of him as his real father. I don't go through Tulsa anymore." When he talked about this part of his life, it was the only time the smile left Dave's face. Is the woman in Tulsa bitter, is she better off now, does Randy Bob feel lost, abandoned, did he inherit nomad genes? Dave looked like the kind of father who would have doted, but because he never knew his own parents, because from his standpoint they split on him, perhaps that's the only kind of father he knows how to be.

Lunching a table away from Denver Dave in the Bangor soup kitchen one day, Anna Maria Caprozano and her six-year-old daughter constitute a family unit that has included child abuse, child neglect, incest, truancy, and wife beating. To begin with, Mrs. Caprozano, a 33-year-old with beautiful long black hair, dirt under her nails, and very tired eyes, hits her child for almost anything. "Get ya hands off them rolls, Kid, or I'll slap ya blue." She also leaves her daughter Sophia, whom everyone calls "Kid," alone in a tiny walkup while she's out, often all day. She does not send Kid to school, moving frequently to avoid Kid's father.

After being told several times she'd be smacked for touching a roll or reaching for a second piece of apple pie, Kid looked up at her mother carefully, trying to read her. Was Anna Maria really in a good mood or was she really mad? Will the smack just sting my fanny or will it make by cheeks puffy?

Anna Maria Caprozano appeared to see her parenthood as an

impediment that could be occasionally pleasurable. Because Kid was always getting into things, Anna Maria told me, the only way to control her was to hit her. Anna Maria and Billy, her boyfriend, took care of Kid in their one-room apartment on a Bangor street lined with shabby Victorian relics, but she was planning on leaving to stay a step ahead of her ex-husband. Kid's father wouldn't stay with Anna Maria and his daughter, but neither would he leave them alone. "He blows in and out of Maine," she told me, "looking for easy work and easy women. When he's around he acts like we have to do anything he says. If we move now it's going to be harder for her father to find us." Between Maine and Massachusetts, they had lived six places in the past year. Kid's father had a tendency to be violent. Once he had broken into a place of Anna Maria's in Massachusetts. Her boyfriend Billy had tried to protect Anna Maria, but her ex-husband overpowered him and then beat up Anna Maria with a clothes hanger. That time he never touched Kid, though. "I do that myself, it's the only language Kid understands. She's as ornery as her father, can't you see that? Youngsters these days, they need a little more strictness. Billy don't raise a hand to her, so I have to."

Anna Maria told me her own background was "checkered." That turned out to mean she was raised by a mother who brought home a succession of "sort-of stepfathers, none too bad, none too good." The stepfathers never bothered Anna Maria sexually. "That was left to two of my uncles, may they rot in hell. Came on to me the same night when I was 14. I still remember how they stunk, and how I did when they were through with me." As we talked outside the Salvation Army, Billy came back from an errand with Kid on his shoulders. The two of them were laughing, pretending Billy was a bucking bronco and Kid his rider. "Let's get packed," Anna Maria said, looking up at her six-year-old daughter on her boyfriend's shoulders. "I want to get out of that room before your stupid father shows up. If he catches up with us again, I got half a mind to let him have you."

"Please, mama, no," Kid said. She knew how her father treated her mother and must have believed he'd hit Kid much worse than her mother does if she tried to live with him. Kid was perched on her boyfriend Billy, but Anna Maria behaved as if the child were on her own shoulders, a burden to be borne.

"Then let's hit the road," she said. "I can go a lot faster without you so get a move on if you're sticking with me." Kid wriggled down from Billy's shoulders and was clinging to her mother's hand as the three of them hurried away from the Salvation Army building. They must have moved quickly because I never saw them again around Bangor.

At the other end of the spectrum from Anna Maria among the underclass mothers I met in Bangor was Adriana Saint Duclos Mathere. While Anna Maria lived with a daughter she appeared to want only sporadically, Adriana no longer lived with two children she missed desperately. Anna Maria felt hobbled, encumbered, by having to raise a child who reminded her of a former husband she had come to detest. Adriana had lost her children, somewhat like Ronnielee Divine in Oakland, when in the judgment of others she could no longer properly care for them. Like Ronnielee, Adriana found her loss heartbreaking.

Whenever she talked about her motherhood, about the two children but who are no longer with her, Adriana would look happy and sad simultaneously. She loved recalling her children; she hated not being with them. Her deepest sorrow, as she struggled from a state hovering near extreme want to something approaching genteel poverty, was not being with her children. "My son became very ill, and right then my family became downwardly mobile," she said as we walked around her Bangor neighborhood near the Salvation Army kitchen. "The insurance—I call it *un*surance—covered almost nothing. My poor husband struggled, and I struggled, and our two kids struggled." Her son eventually got well, but Adriana said she unraveled during the boy's illness, and her breakdown was the opportunity her in-laws had been waiting for to get their son and grandchildren away from her. "Their sweet, weak father is all right," Adriana said, "but I ache when I think about my two kids, nine and six now. I see them weekends, not every weekend but sometimes. They aren't as poor as I am—a $135-a-month dump above a cleaner, yuck—but they're lonely. Me, too. It's indescribable, the pain for your kids when you don't see them ride their first two-wheeler, or in their Halloween costumes."

Adriana took stock, looking around her at the shabby homes grayly squatting together along her street. She knew she was no middle-class housewife who happened to lose a tough custody battle. She was not angry at her ex-husband. She knew who she was and where she was. "I sure wouldn't want my children around the types in this neighborhood," she said, "especially the ones who come over to the soup kitchen. Those bums are slummy in their heads. But I can't offer my kids anything better now. That's a good reason they're with their father. That's a better reason they're not with me."

In Oakland, Ronnielee Divine, the fidgety, eager-to-please Jamaican whose youngest children were taken from her for 18 months while she fought off cocaine, will do anything to avoid losing them another time. With no job, she finds most of her identity in her parenthood. With no steady boyfriend, most of her pleasure also comes from her children. It happened to be Christmas Eve when her prim social worker informed Ronnielee she was now judged competent to have her children returned to her. " 'This is highly unorthodox and under the circumstances highly provisional,' " Ronnielee quoted the social worker as saying. "Big college words, you know," she added.

Ronnielee went on to tell me how stunned she was. She fell to her knees in front of the social worker, crying and praying at the same time. "Christmas, Christmas, Christmas, sweet Jesus, I was so happy!" she said. The social worker, whom Ronnielee described as a middle-class black woman, was embarrassed. "I know I was treating her like God, but I was just so happy, so thankful. I'd lie, cheat, beg, steal, or hustle to keep hold of my kids." Several times in talking to me Ronnielee repeated the resonant phrase "never again." Shadowed by the memory of her addiction, Ronnielee inches her way toward the working class, an underclass mother who wants more for her children than she herself has ever had. The fierceness with which she hangs on to her children overrides all her subordinate needs. "They took them once, I was in hell," she said, "and before anyone takes them now, they're gonna have to tie me, whip me, and starve me. Never again."

The mere fact of underclass mothers staying with underclass children, whether with the intensity of Ronnielee Divine or the resentment of Anna Maria Caprozano, hardly solves the problem of how a new generation can be raised to transcend the problems that surround the old. In my travels I was more perplexed by the replication of the underclass, from parent to child, than by even the wretched conditions of underclass life itself. The best programs I saw for breaking the underclass cycle were at the Parent Child Center on the South Side of Chicago and at Avancé in San Antonio. In addition to the care given to babies, toddlers, and Head Start children, the South Side PCC becomes a social focus for parents. A staff of 14 handles the 125 children in the three PCC child care levels and offers their parents services that would otherwise be beyond their reach. Parents at the PCC, who often had very little parental attention of their own while growing up in fragmented families, are shown how to communicate with their children without screaming, how to discipline without hitting, how to attend to their own needs without neglecting those of their babies. They are also offered psychological counseling though this service suffered from insufficient visibility among the parents when I was there.

Isolation from the larger community has a tendency to make an underclass existence a life sentence. To combat this, the PCC sponsors excursions to museums, fashion shows, and public parks, where a simple middle-class activity such as a picnic becomes a revelation to an underclass parent. While not providing specific vocational training, the PCC's staff explores ways for parents to complete their education and find jobs. Self-expression and a sense of competence, unprecedented in the lives of many of the parents, are encouraged during workshops in arts and crafts. Sessions on family planning and stress management allow parents to get to know each other in a peaceful setting removed from the tension of the projects where most of them live. But I repeat the word "parents" here, unfortunately, as a euphemism the PCC's own staff used while speaking to me. I saw only mothers at the center, and the PCC does not have the money to send representatives out into the projects to persuade fathers to be fathers.

Dinah Lou Freeman, who had told me the parable of the two tables as her explanation of how children are initiated into drugs, uses the PCC as an antidote to the neighborhood. "You teach *your* kids possibilities," she told me. "*I* teach *mine* to be scared. At the PCC at least they can be curious without paying too high a price." She receives AFDC for all three boys and Social Security for Louis and Gabriel, the two eldest ones. I asked why the Social Security at such a tender age. "That's because their father Henry was murdered."

Whether she paused for effect or because of the painful recollection, Dinah Lou's tale became more memorable alongside her looks. Her complexion is a rich mocha, and her short hair comes down into a widow's peak high on her forehead. Wide, questioning eyes enhance the proportioned sensuality of her nose and mouth. Her smooth contoured lips are like those on a Cambodian statue, and she wears no lipstick nor any other makeup. She knows enough about her natural resources to set them off with a black turtleneck that gives you nothing to look at but her striking features.

"There was a lot of animosity in the family of Louis and Gabriel's father, Henry," she said so quietly I had to strain to hear her. "He went up to Wisconsin to see them and he had already bought his bus ticket back home when it happened. I was six months pregnant with Gabriel at the time. We had lived together four years, not ready for marriage. I was taking it one day at a time, because there were many family problems on his side. Actually, he was depressed. Something that might go wrong would really put him down. But we loved each other very much. I still don't see how I'm going to tell the older boys about their father. The police found him shot by the side of the road, no gun anywhere though it could have been stolen, the receipt for a bus ticket in his pocket. He was 20."

Why would she expect a gun to be found near the body of a man shot by someone else? I took her mention of both depression and family trouble to mean that Dinah Lou was ruling out neither suicide nor murder. When I pressed further, she said simply, "It was just mysterious, Henry's passing." It made little difference. An unexplained death to the police meant a loverless, fatherless home for her and her children. Dinah Lou was 20 when Henry was killed. Growing up, she had met her own father only a few times and at the age of three was given over by her mother to her grandmother. "My mother raised the three other children she had, each one by a different father," she recalled. "'Why not me? Why didn't she raise me, too?' is what I never could stop asking myself." She hadn't found the answer to that question when I met her. Dinah Lou remembered seeing her father once when she was about seven. He brought her a jack-in-the-box for Christmas. When the jack-in-the-box flew up in her face, scaring Dinah Lou, her father couldn't stop laughing, which scared Dinah Lou more. She was frightened until he finally left. Dinah Lou surmised that perhaps her mother hadn't liked her father much, and that was why she gave up Dinah Lou to be raised by a grandmother.

Supporting herself as a cashier at McDonald's, Burger King, Walgreens, and gas stations, Dinah Lou had been a high school honors student and was eventually hired to tutor seventh-graders in math and reading comprehension. She finished one year of college. After Henry's death she stopped work and quit college, demoralized and unable to afford babysitters.

Putting her children first, Dinah Lou took them everywhere she went. "I'm never not with them, which is good," she said, "but sometimes I wonder when I'm going to get to be something for myself." A year after Henry's death she met another man, Seward, who works as a cook's assistant in a hospital. The following year she had her third son, Marvin. She and Seward have remained a couple though they don't yet live together because she's afraid of losing her AFDC payments if a man is found at her apartment.

In her housing project she is surrounded by drugs "on the stairway, in the hallway, on the first floor, a lot of the mothers selling their babies' milk for a hit." Not to mention the two tables in the gang's apartment upstairs where, she had told me, candy is dispensed at the first and drugs at the second. Dinah Lou has what she calls her 10-year outline. When her baby turns three and can attend Head Start by himself, she wants to take courses in electronics with the hope of starting her own maintenance business. "I know I have to work in someone else's shop first," she said, "but I'll be aiming higher. I want to be on my own. By the 10th year I'll have my own business. Seward and I will be married, nice home in the suburbs. My older boys, Henry's children, already call Seward 'Daddy.' "

Dinah Lou is better educated than most of the other mothers at the PCC. She helps the others read about job openings and has enrolled in a computer training class. Her next goal is to take a television repair course. The PCC does not have organized classes, only group sessions on almost any subject the mothers care to discuss. A staff member told me that most of the mothers coming to the PCC, including those with nominal degrees from high school, read at only about a sixth-grade level. They need far more remedial education than Dinah Lou does to qualify for even the lowest-paying jobs. Yet in other ways Dinah Lou is typical of both the background and foreground of the welfare mothers I met. Neglected at the beginning of their own lives, they made babies early and didn't find out who they were or what they wanted until they were already mothers of several children. Climbing out of their teens at last, they look around and see the economic and geographic snare they're in. They have no money and no way of going anyplace where they could get some. At that point they either surrender to idleness or drugs, or, like Dinah Lou, lay plans for an escape.

At the Chicago PCC, the chief concern remains children, who also are the beneficiaries of the most highly organized programs for infants, toddlers, and Head Start youngsters. The Avancé centers in San Antonio provide an atmosphere more oriented to parents' needs. Richard Zorolla, a highly motivated social worker who manages an Avancé program, is sponsoring classes in adult literacy, nutrition, toymaking, and family planning as well as the full range of child development activities offered at the PCC. He has won the respect of barrio teenagers by coaching basketball. Possessing a rare combination of idealism and pragmatism, Zorolla is an administrator who is dynamic as well as poised. When looking at the multitudes of problems ghetto and barrio agencies face, and the bureaucracies that bury the problems in paperwork, I was always impressed with anyone who is unsatisfied and impatient to do more.

Zorolla does not want to address only the needs of children but those of their parents as well. He concentrates in particular on the psychological environment and moods of underclass parents. Again, as in Chicago, "parents" is a euphemism because few fathers show up at the Avancé programs. This neglect is not peculiar to black and Hispanic fathers; of the white Anglo Saxon fathers I spoke to in Bangor and Los Angeles, not a single one was paying any consistent attention to his children. As with other aspects of underclass existence, I found economic, educational, and emotional issues prevailing over racial and ethnic distinctions. It is the emotional issues that especially interest Richard Zorolla.

In augmenting the adult program at Avancé, Zorolla was preparing to offer group therapy and individual psychotherapy. He was indignant over what he saw as the cavalier dismissal of underclass psychological problems by middle-class people who find those same problems disabling in their own lives. "We haven't even begun to consider how much depression there is among the very poor," he told me. "We don't seem to think they have a right, or the ability, to feel deeply enough. The mental health needs of the women who come in here are staggering. This is true of men, too, but we don't see them enough to make accurate estimates. Because of poverty's accompanying conditions of neglect, deprivation, and the drugs everywhere, the emotional issues of the very poor simply haven't been addressed. A lot of mothers are verging on clinical depression and just stop coming in. The socioeconomic situation alone is depressing—the environment overwhelms them. There's no father in the house, they have five children, and maybe one of the kids has a major health or discipline problem. Who wouldn't be depressed? We want to reach out to them, but so far we haven't had the money to do that. We *have* to find it somewhere!"

Zorolla's perception of the community's pain was matched by his resolve to alleviate it. This was not matched by a commitment from the larger community—private, municipal, state, or federal. Wealthy Texans have been exuberantly generous in their support for the arts, but Avancé and its sister agencies essentially have to beg to get private donations. Both the city of San Antonio and the state government have felt a general Texas pinch since the late '80s, and poverty programs with their virtually powerless constituencies are always the first to suffer. On the national level, the Clinton campaign pledge to "end welfare as we know it" had led, as 1994 slid from the hands of journalists into those of historians, only to a poverty dead-lock between Congress and the administration. What the national uncertainties translate into in a single Hispanic neighborhood in San Antonio, if you're Richard Zorolla of Avancé, is good intentions, no consistency, and not much followthrough.

I was given permission to sit in on the Avancé class in family planning, which, because many of the students are teenagers, amounts largely to sex education. It was an all-female class. The young women tittered when I presented myself at the classroom door, and the teacher asked me to wait outside while she completed her condom instruction. More giggles. As the teacher gave her how-to demonstration, a tidal wave of laughter swept toward me under the door.

When I was allowed into the classroom, the teacher, an early middle-aged woman named Emma Garza, was telling the class to make sure they give contraceptive instructions to their own daughters as soon as the daughters can understand. Mrs. Garza had enough vitality for half a dozen 20-year-olds, teaching with humor, example, and goad. Promoters of abstinence would label her polit-ically incorrect, but I found her refreshingly realistic. "Now, let's talk about your darling innocent little girls. Do they have sex at 12?

Well, I do, and I'm a grandmother. Why not just assume that people who can have sex *will* have sex? Teach them, teach them!"

A woman asked if contraceptive pills can cause cancer. Another wanted to know if they would make her fat. Mrs. Garza emphasized that the pills don't cause cancer but can lead to weight gain, and if that's a concern she advised them to use another method. She cautioned them all to have pap smears. "We have a lot of Hispanic women dying of cancer of the uterus because they neglected to have pap smears." She explained ovulation as if she were talking to eighth-graders, which in a couple of instances looked to be the case. When asked about surgical methods of birth control, she described tubal ligation for women and sterilization for men, but added that even these don't always work and are frequently irreversible if people change their minds.

Mrs. Garza wound her way around the contraceptive track until she came back to the pill. She warned her class that many women share their pills, and she emphasized this doesn't work. "All that will happen if you share with a friend is *both* of you will get pregnant. The man's sperm can live five days, a quick five seconds and you're pregnant. You have to be regular about taking the pill, and if you're using this method you should take it the same time every day."

A nervous young woman put up her hand. "I went to work Monday and I left my job at 5:30. Usually I go straight home and take the pill at 6:00, but I didn't go home Monday." She paused, with a weight on her shoulders that she finally unloaded by blurting: "Monday night me and him got together and you know . . ."

"You mean you had intercourse, Teofila?" Mrs. Garza asked.

"Um, Monday night me and him got together . . ."

"You're talking about intercourse."

"Uh, yeah, I mean he usually pulls out but this time he doesn't pull out, he leaves his stuff inside. I came back home and took the pill. Maybe it was midnight then."

A few giggles. Everyone had been where Teofila had been.

"No good," Mrs. Garza said. "You take the pill the same time every day, and you don't lock the barn door after the horse is stolen."

Teofila started counting the fingers on her left hand with her right index finger. She counted them three times, then gave a worried look at Emma Garza. "So it's like 15 days since my last period started. I'm right in the middle. Am I pregnant?"

"I hope not, Teofila," Mrs. Garza said. "But hope isn't good enough. Next month I don't want to have to *hope* you're not pregnant. I want to *know* you're not—or as close as possible to knowing. No more leaving the barn door open. Okay, Teofila?"

Teofila nodded, blinking rapidly, looking worried. The class broke up with cheerful resolutions among the young women that were all variations on the old injunction to be good and if you can't be good, be careful. I remembered that in Chicago I had seen women in a group called Parents Too Soon trying to lock doors after a whole stable is emptied. Avancé is trying to preempt the need for Parents Too Soon, but of course many of the women there have already become mothers. The counseling and parental training that Avancé gives mothers offer the merest beginning of what could lift a fatherless family out of the underclass quicksand.

Avancé's surveys are an accurate match with national statistics. A third of the adolescents who give birth already have at least one child. Children provide meaning in an underclass life that has very little of it anywhere else. Bearing a child is a source of pride and love, and a baby gives immediate purpose to its mother. But the purpose is blunted, deflected, when the environment is mined with underclass traps. It seems to be a social axiom that becoming the underclass parent of an underclass child is an almost precise algebraic formula for increasing the size of the underclass geometrically. I thought the Avancé approach was effective because I thought Emma Garza was effective. It appeared hopeful that among Mexican-Americans whose religious training has often equated birth control with sin there was an Hispanic teacher outspoken in her advocacy of contraception.

I have already noted the problems of underclass fathers as fathers.

They are encouraged by welfare rules and their own humiliating nonposition in society to abandon the women and children who would in other classes constitute their families. When I was able to corner an underclass father long enough to talk about his fatherhood, he was often only slightly more paternal than Hector Zacario. I would run into three responses from fathers: shame, defiance, apathy.

Sometimes all three responses came from the same man, which was true of Federico Morales in the Alazan Apache Courts. "Damn," he led with, "I hate myself so much every time I think about it. Me, a deadbeat dad. Ugh, you know?" I couldn't tell how deeply he meant this or how rehearsed he may have been for the occasional social worker or priest he might bump into. He was not sure whether he had three children or four. My questions about the mothers of his children led to the second response, defiance. "They want the babies, let *them* take care of them. How many ladies I get pregnant? Two I think, maybe three. But I'm not looking for no babies, I told them that, like the first time I was with them, from the get-go. I'm out of work since '93, what do I need a baby for? Hell with the ladies, hell with their babies, man."

The third response, apathy, surfaced when we had talked for a while. "Oh man, gimme a break, what can I do anyway?" Federico Morales said to himself as much as to me. "I come around to see one of these ladies a week ago. Maybe take the kids for an ice cream. She shoos me off. 'They see you here I lose my welfare,' she says. So I split, like I get lost. That's where I am, man, lost. Fuck it, you know?" Federico's family has lived in Texas for three generations, and each generation has alternated between welfare and menial jobs that don't last. He had nothing going for him and never had. When his apathy was spent, Federico began again with his first response, shame. "Oh yeah, man, I wish I would be a father to my kids. I could see them on weekends when the welfare don't come around, I've done that some. I don't know why I don't do it more. I meant to last Sunday, but my buddy shows up with a half-gallon of California red, you know. Just write I'm a total waste, man, a total shit."

With this cue, a buddy of Federico's did mosey by. Tall, angular, bent, drunk, a torn ear. Federico motioned him over. It was Hector Zacario. Federico Morales looked to his older friend as an authority. "Hey, Zacario, tell this guy about the kids *you* got."

Hector Zacario did not remember me. "What's this fuck want?" he asked. Then he did remember me, in his way. "Oh, I know you, you fuck."

Perhaps Hector Zacario sized me up for an agent of some temporal power he was trying to elude. Collecting his cans and bottles for redemption at the nearest 7-11, he had told me he was the great redeemer. In this case, he wasn't collecting, and it would have taken a broad pentecostal stretch to regard him as either redeeming or redeemed. "What you want?" he asked, but he wasn't interested in the answer any more than he was interested in further questions. "What I do's what I do," he said, a declaration as final as it was circular, as circular as his whole existence. "Fuck anyone who wants to know about my kids. I see them, that's my business. I don't see them, that's my business too. Why don't you and Mr. Anglo go take a flying fuck, Federico?"

7

Old and Poor

Where You Are
Is Where You Stay

Old age is our emotional capstone. It crowns the arch of our lives pointedly and poignantly—or else it fails, with equal point and poignance, to provide that crown. In "The Death of the Hired Man," Robert Frost wrote that the impoverished old day laborer had "nothing to look backward to with pride, / And nothing to look forward to with hope." Wherever I went among the elderly underclass I was struck by the almost tangible weight that frequently hangs on the condition of being old and poor. One morning in Oakland I was talking to a social worker at a poverty agency when an elderly woman hobbled in using a cane. The room instantly seemed to become heavier. While she was receiving the permission she wanted to eat lunch early, an old man shambled in, coughing and wheezing, spitting tobacco juice into a Dixie cup he carried, and now the room became heavier still. The old man only wanted an aspirin.

They were not a couple, the social worker told me. Each of them was not only old and poor, a lethal enough combination, but also alone. When they had gone their separate ways to the single-room-occupancy hotels they lived in, the social worker said it was no use examining the causes of their problems and how these might be redressed because rehabilitation was no longer the issue for them or for those who wanted to help them. The issue was simply making them less uncomfortable, making their last days bearable. Alleviate their distress, don't kid them about becoming productive members of society because most of them never were in the first place.

The social worker was looking away too soon, as many doctors do, from the elderly, but I saw what he saw before he looked away. It was desolation. The elderly are fond of looking back: the longer they live, the longer their memory stretches, the shorter their anticipations. But the elderly among the underclass are coming to the end, often alone, with little to recall that has provided them with more than regret. They may have multiplied, as the Bible enjoins, but they haven't been particularly fruitful. And those they have produced in their multiplication have little to thank them for.

We like to think we enrich the earth by our presence. Our lives have meaning in proportion to the truths we find, truths that become our legacies. We leave behind children, works, ideas, a garden, a home, a tradition for grandchildren to inherit. The elderly find solace as the end approaches in looking back on the more fulfilling times in their lives, especially on having created new people they are proud of and who will carry on their identity in diverse ways. Looking back on an underclass life is often like looking back on a desert, with a daunting psychological destitution to match the material condition.

"You can be young without money but you can't be old without it," Maggie tells her husband Brick in Tennessee Williams' *Cat on a Hot Tin Roof,* "because to be old without it is just too awful." It may be awful, and the combination of age and poverty is a central fear in our society, but it is a condition that 4 million Americans over the age of 65 have to endure. Maggie had a far higher standard of what constitutes poverty than the federal government has, but her attitude is shared by the poor as well as the middle class. The elderly poor tend not to think of themselves, or to be thought of by their younger fellow citizens, as employable, which makes their condition unlikely to change in good times or bad. The corps of old and poor have had lives that form a kind of inverted history, a past seen from the bottom, of the last three generations of Americans.

The old and poor are by no means uniformly sad. It should not stop us from helping ease later years that are hardly golden, but I had no trouble finding exceptions among the elderly poor who would describe themselves as independent and ornery. They carried the weight of their poverty much more comfortably than those who had surrendered to both their infirmities and their solitude. Approaching his own old age, William Butler Yeats included a cautionary passage in a poem full of yearning and mystery, "Sailing to Byzantium":

> An aged man is but a paltry thing,
> A tattered coat upon a stick, unless
> Soul clap its hands and sing, and louder sing
> For every tatter in its mortal dress.

The poet might have looked fondly on the flavor—of reminiscence, drink, fellowship—that Banjo Horace puts into his old age.

Banjo Horace is elderly and poor in Oakland, unshy about proclaiming his faith in liquor to preserve him from becoming an elderly poor corpse. Starting out as a boy running moonshine in Vicksburg, Banjo Horace, as he is called when he isn't called Horace the Plucker, was a stevedore on the docks in New Orleans until he was 26, rode the rails from Los Angeles to Atlanta until he was 35, drove a small poultry truck in Seattle until he had too many drunk driving arrests at 44, and now, at 76, lives in a skid row hotel in Oakland.

Horace doesn't get a pension because he never worked anywhere long enough to qualify, but he does get Social Security and some Supplemental Security Income (SSI), the latter based on an old back injury sustained when he jumped off a freight train to escape some hoboes who were trying to roll him. These days he drinks and plays his banjo. Yeats would be proud of him: He is no tattered paltry thing, he does clap and sing. The single-room-occupancy hotel he lives in is a downtown flophouse that once was used for railway workers during Oakland layovers. Banjo Horace is undaunted by his surroundings. "Get in here!" he yells at anyone passing his room. "The story of my life is the story of America the Beautiful. We grew up together, we're growing old together. Let me tell you about the time I woke up next to a strawberry blonde in Tupelo . . . " And he starts, sometimes with a story, sometimes with a song he accompanies on his banjo. Banjo Horace is never reticent.

Many years ago I knew Katie Sheetz in Los Angeles, a 78-year-old with a granddaughter who sometimes visited her one-room walkup but couldn't afford to help with anything more than an occasional bag of groceries. A decade after that, when Ralph Ruiz was still in his priestly incarnation, he introduced me to Acapito Landeros in San Antonio. With a face resembling an enlarged walnut, eyes growing dimmer each week, Acapito Landeros often accidentally mixed cockroaches into the rice and beans he cooked for himself over a Sterno can twice a day in his barrio hovel. Both Katie and Acapito had medical needs that would devastate middle-class families and that made them, as they grew older and more feeble, virtual wards of their counties. Old age is almost always lonely in a country that worships youth, far lonelier when you are destitute.

It is also true, however, that old age has drawn our national sympathies, even if we like to keep our distance from those we regard as infected by it. We have helped the aged financially more than we have helped any other age group. If they were still alive, Katie Sheetz and Acapito Landeros might be much better off today. Proportionately, there are fewer aged poor in America than there ever were. The poverty rate for the elderly dropped from 35.2 percent in 1959 to 12.9 percent in 1992. Medicare, one of the Great Society's most significant victories in its war on poverty, now makes many of the illnesses of old age at least bearable economically. Though threatened by the budget deficits of the '90s, Medicare endured as one program that worked. Poverty specialists argue that social spending in the past 25 years has gone disproportionately to the elderly. In 1990 the government spent $353 billion on Medicare and Social Security, but only $100 billion for the programs—including food stamps, school lunches, tax credits, Medicaid, Aid to Families with

Dependent Children, and all other forms of welfare—that help the nonelderly poor. Perhaps because the elderly still vote, perhaps because we're all headed in their direction, our society takes better care of the aged, fiscally if not emotionally, than any other segment of the population.

The lot of the aged poor is cushioned, but no one has figured out how to use them, how to reclaim productive roles for them in our culture. While this is true of retired people in general—the elderly nonpoor—there are programs that draw on the experience of middle-class retirees by placing them in training positions in their former companies. Other middle-class programs bring the very old and the very young together, with the elderly enriching children by reading to them and telling them stories. In turn the children provide the elderly with energy and a reason to carry on. It's a decent trade. But for the elderly poor, old age is no culmination, only an affirmation of uselessness, an anticlimax to a life that has held few enough climactic moments even in its supposed prime. As medical advances continue to keep more people alive longer, the elderly poor will inevitably proliferate, and a lonely, uncomfortable, and meaningless time in many of their lives will simply be extended. For the aging underclass, the future looks even worse than the present. It is the future that bedevils Hastings Howell.

Though he has frequent aches, 72-year-old Hastings Howell needs nothing so much as to be needed. Old and alone, homeless, widowed, he waited for his free lunch one noontime in Bangor. In the late winter cold he wore a green cap and a zipped wool jacket that looked somewhat porous; his eyes were rheumy and he sniffled a bit. "It's not so bad," he said, referring to both the weather and his cold. "Bad is I don't know where my grandchildren are. Bad is I lost my wife a year ago. She was my third, the other two went their own ways. But her dying, that's what bad is, isn't it?" Hastings Howell's look of gloom was increased by the downward set of his features, which were gathered near the center of his face as if summoned by a force of nature that abhorred expansiveness. Under his cap, his white hair still showed traces of the sandy red he had sported in his prime.

The work Hastings Howell had done was work that an eighth-grade dropout of his generation, starting out in Lowell, Massachusetts, might be expected to find. He spent nine years in the army, first as a driver and later as a cook; he was a gandy dancer on a railroad section crew; a cook's helper in a restaurant; a housepainter; a nursing home attendant; a garbage man; and finally a grave digger. Grave digging has often become a last-resort job among unskilled laborers. Sooner or later, it seemed, many of the elderly men I met in Hastings Howell's position, or lack of position, would find themselves putting other people in the ground. Wending his way through jobs and joblessness, on the margins of respectable poverty, he lost track of his children and stepchildren. Unsure of himself, Hastings Howell seldom made an assertion unless he followed it with a question. "I'd like to see some grandkids, though," he said. "I might could tell them a thing or two, don't you think?"

Since his last wife's death Hastings Howell has tried to kill himself several times. "Once I took my wife's cancer pills, and they did make me feel pretty awful," he said, chuckling bitterly, "but then I settled on booze and I've done a lot of that. The last time I tried, I slit my wrists. Night watchman found me. Why'd he bother?"

Gloomy as he was, Hastings Howell was still a romantic. He told me he had fallen for a woman little better off than he, just as remote from family, and just as lonely. "I need someone I can cuddle up to, talk to, wait on," he said. "I love to wait on a woman I love. Why not Daphne?" He perked up when he said Daphne's name. He became hopeful. Daphne was very poor, too, but she had an apartment that Social Security paid for, and she ate there, not at the soup kitchen. "By Jeez, I think I'll go pay her a call after lunch. She's a good old girl herself. Make some plans with her. You think Daphne will have me?" As he slurped some gummy chicken noodle soup, too much of which ended up on his chin, I couldn't think of anything kinder than to wish Hastings Howell good luck with Daphne.

Wherever I have looked at the elderly poor, confined by the isolation of age, its own inescapable ghetto, they have displayed their own array of strategies for survival. Near the close of a lifetime some are homeless, some are in slums, some are in projects that have become slums. Regardless of their conditions of shelter, homelessness is not as much of a problem as hopelessness. Those who are near their families, particularly the younger generation in their families, have seemed to me to be measurably—I almost want to say immeasurably—better off than the aged who are hived away by themselves.

In the Alazan Apache Courts in San Antonio, Carlos Espinosa has been officially disabled for 21 years since he fell off a rack in the frozen food–processing plant where he worked. He walks almost without a limp, proudly fixes anything that breaks in his apartment, and drives easily, but he says his back has never been any good since his accident. Miguel Espinosa, the five-year-old Alazan Apache boy I met who has weak legs and an undernourished look, is Carlos Espinosa's grandson, and Miguel's mother Mercedes, who worries about the sprayheads in the projects, is Carlos's daughter. Miguel brings the family AFDC, Mercedes gets food stamps, and Carlos draws a government disability check along with Social Security.

"You have the operation on your back," Carlos Espinosa said, "and the operation doesn't help, and you think I've done my work so I can move around here and there in the projects, help my wife in the house. See my grandchildren raised right." What he meant by the last remark was that he and his wife are bringing up three of their grandchildren because Carlos Espinosa didn't like the way one of his six daughters was doing the job. The daughter, I was told by another resident in Alazan Apache, had become a sprayhead and then graduated to harder drugs, hustling to pay for them. In three generations the Espinosas of Alazan Apache are not breaking the poverty cycle, but the grandparents are at least attached to the family, providing the offspring of a wayward child with stability. The grandchildren are providing the elder Espinosas with a purpose.

Washed up on the Santa Monica Pier, white-maned Rainey Fitzwilliam Gibbs, as he carefully enunciated his three names, no longer saw himself as having a purpose. He said he worked his whole life, more on than off, until he couldn't take the routine anymore.

"Thirty-eight years a carpenter in Little Rock, Arkansas," he told me, "and then I hit the skids. Tossed overboard I was, disgusted with everybody, everybody disgusted with me." He said he didn't begin to drink heavily until he lost his job, and soon he lost everything else. "Kids wouldn't speak to me. Wife asked me one day as I went for the door, 'When you coming home?' I said, 'I ain't got no home,' and that was pretty much it. I got nothing now. Just my name." Again he intoned, as if to reassure himself, his first, middle, and last names.

He lurches from drink to shelter to beach to senior center to the street again. Listening to him, I couldn't say Rainey Fitzwilliam Gibbs belongs in a hospital, a conventional retirement community, or back with the family he walked out on. A residential center for drifters would be, after all, a contradiction in terms. It did occur to me that there should be some spot he could call home, some singular place, as Robert Frost wrote of the old farmhand, "where, when you have to go there, / They have to take you in." But not all social ills find public remedies. Even the most well-meant comfort station might be resisted by Rainey Fitzwilliam Gibbs at twilight.

I was talking to one old man on Cahuenga Boulevard in Hollywood when another old man challenged me: "What are you doing standing there, all young and wealthy?" It did not matter that I felt neither young nor rich, that I felt in fact quite wilted and needy near the end of another day searching out the stories and privations of people like himself. But he was right. I could, as I have pointed out before, escape any time. Here, the truth lay in perception, and Richard Downes, my questioner, accurately perceived me as a good deal younger and less needy than he. Richard Downes stands outside a restaurant in Hollywood and opens the door for patrons. It is not one of the better Hollywood restaurants or they would have hired someone to do that, and someone else to park Mercedes and shoo away old fellows like Richard Downes. But it is one of the kinder restaurants; the assistant manager hands Richard Downes a cardboard box of leftovers three or four times a day, receiving in return a low bow from the bald old man. After he asked me what I was doing, Richard Downes began hacking uncontrollably.

"Oh man," Richard Downes said as night came on, bringing a chill to Southern California, "I'm coffin up flame." He did not pause long enough for me to ask if his insides were on fire or if he meant phlegm. He was aiming at a contrast to which he had now turned his attention, the elderly poor with the elderly rich. "Jack Warner came into the Beverly Hills Medical Center when I was a lowly attendant there. The picture tycoon. Now *there* was an old man who lived right. 'Course he was a vegetable by the time I knew him, couldn't move by himself, couldn't talk. But a real tycoon to the end. Had the same barber for 35 years, fellow would come every week to shave and trim Jack. It wasn't long after Jack passed that I went to prison for manslaughter. Fight in a bar got out of hand."

A grandfather several times, Richard Downes has a daughter who is 49, a son 47. He hasn't seen either of them since he left prison five years ago. Brought up in a Brooklyn orphanage, he married a woman from Virginia, left her to join the Seabees during World War II, worked on a railroad in Wyoming, and did typewriter repair in Las Vegas before sliding down to Los Angeles to land odd jobs such as the one in the medical center that housed Jack Warner. "Where I made my mistake," he said in almost amused reflection, "was skipping out on the old lady. Her father was a vice president of Continental Can until the booze got him, but he still had dough. He was a big Mason, too. They take care of their own. I fixed things so nobody's taking care of me." Richard Downes was ending up as he'd started out, effectively orphaned.

I went home to Maine from California, feeling grim about the plight of the aged poor. Their own fatalism had surely been contagious. Old age is often sentimentalized, and I was in no mood for that. The elderly are intrinsically no more noble than the rest of us. Not everything old is an antique. Sheer endurance may be worthy of some admiration, not of reverence. California left me with the certainty that the newer parts of the country were handling the underclass elderly no better than the old. At least in the Bangor shelter I felt by now an adoptive kinship.

A month after I saw him at the soup kitchen, when he had been determined to press his courtship of the lady named Daphne, Hastings Howell shuffled into the Bangor shelter. As dilapidated as he was, the sight of the old man raised my spirits. However sad their tales or low their estate, the underclass elderly were reminders that life does go on and on, right up to the moment that it does not. Hastings Howell's notions about Daphne not only had given him a hope of becoming un-alone when I'd spoken to him at the soup kitchen but also the possibility of romance. Now, in the shelter, he was red-eyed but sober. I thought perhaps something might have turned for him. I asked what was happening.

He took off a shoe that had no laces and began to shine it on the sleeve of his coat. "She gave me the gate," he said. "I scored some chocolates off a dumpster outside the candy store. Stale, I guess, but still looking like they're in a magazine. I went to see Daphne, took her the chocolates. She was cordial at first. Greeted me in that dignified manner I fell for. 'Oh thank you, kind sir,' said my Daphne. We began our chitchat on terms of extreme amiability. But when we got down to business she couldn't make the commitment. 'Let's back off a bit, Hastings.' How she put it. Basically, she told me to get lost."

He looked over at Kelso Dana, Jr. who still used the shelter from time to time as a kind of home away from the horrific home of his childhood. He was long gone from that home, of course, but he still bounced from apartment to rented room to the shelter, and he was currently homeless. Kelso was showing off his late-model white false teeth to a stranger from Nashville who was hoping to make it small in Bangor. The two paid no attention to the old man. "Wished I'd kept me one of them chocolates," Hastings Howell said to no one. He looked in my direction but didn't seem to find me worthy of comment or attention. Then he swept the room with his gaze. He saw the familiars, the regulars, but there was no one he wanted to divulge himself to.

This time I had nothing to offer. Hastings Howell might find more chocolates and another Daphne. Or the first Daphne might change her mind. Or some old friend might come into the shelter who would recognize him and embrace him against what time was doing to him.

I had no more confidence in the fulfillment of these hopes than Hastings Howell himself did.

Hastings Howell is like many others I came to know—old, alone, broke, broken. The needs of the aged poor overlap with those of alcoholics and the mentally ill. Occasionally, all three seemed to merge as I went from projects to slums to streets to shelters. Was I listening to chronicles or delusions? I could not always tell whether a person's misery was due to the ravages of age, alcohol, or illness. Because all the aged poor I saw need supports that the larger community is not providing, I wasn't sure it mattered. Old age, as a character in *Citizen Kane* says, is the one disease you don't look forward to being cured of. But the loneliness of the elderly poor who have lost their families gave a man like Hastings Howell days and nights with little more than the cure to look forward to. Coming to the end alone, with nothing, nothing in front of him nor behind him, he was deprived of both means and meaning.

Hastings Howell could not hide his annoyance any longer. Kelso Dana's horseplay with the stranger from Nashville goaded the old man. The newcomer showed Kelso a card trick and Kelso again showed the newcomer his new teeth. He took them out of his mouth and was suddenly old; he replaced them and was young again. "Magic, right?" he said.

With the clearest sigh of despair I have ever heard, Hastings Howell blinked at Kelso's shining teeth. "You ain't my folks," he said contemptuously to Kelso and the newcomer. "You ain't like havin' my own. My own place. My own people." He turned back to me. "Daphne won't see me. It's all over, isn't it?"

8

Journey's End

I am neither a policy nor a poverty specialist. I took my journey to the very poor, and I know more about this neglected group of Americans than I did before, but I also know the journey was about me as well as about them. I was most aware of the poor, most sensitive to them as individuals and as citizens, when I stopped imposing my fantasies on their reality and simply accepted their reality. My completed journey left me feeling incomplete. After going among the sunken, the caged, and the trapped, I felt both relief and guilt at leaving them behind. I cannot pretend I wish I could trade places with them. Neither could I indifferently walk away.

It is clear that the war on poverty of the '60s has evolved into the war on the poor of the '90s. The so-called Great Society programs had many limitations and faults; they reached very few of the under-class; some of them eroded into dependency cushions. They were intended and directed, however, to combat poverty. There is no such intent or direction in the mid-90s.

The trouble is, it is so much easier to describe problems than to solve them, and the temptation to leave bad enough alone is strong. A writer confronts a social agony, observes it, tries to perfect the pitch of his lamentation, and moves on. I've shown you this mess, he says, and yes, it's terrible, but my job is to illuminate the mess; you figure out how to clean it up. I have every inclination to do exactly that. Observation comes so much more naturally to me than recommendation. But if I'm only a sightseer, I beg the very questions I raise. My journey convinced me that extreme persistent poverty is an extreme persistent problem for everyone, including writers. I had begun, after all, by being mugged.

Although most of the underclass commits no violence, it is not hard to know, from the already numberless muggings and petty crimes as well as from the visible suffering in our midst, what the unmet needs of the very poor are. What is truly difficult is knowing exactly what to do about those needs. Surely the solutions are not simple. Anyone who says the task is easy or that there is a one-size-fits-all remedy is fooling us.

The underclass is composed of people with such diverse problems we might usefully label them the several underclasses instead of trying to corral them all together. In thinking about these diverse problems—deprivation, bias, addiction, instability, retardation, home-lessness, illiteracy—we who do not live in extreme poverty can ask ourselves how far we will travel toward coming up with solutions by just blaming the underclass for their predicament. We know, and the members of the underclass know, that they and we are ranged against each other in American society. Class conflict, the dirty little stifled phrase in America, lurks in every alley and project as surely as it does in suburbs and executive suites.

The threat posed by so many with so little is like a fire alarm going off in our midst. At every age, at every stage of their development, the underclass is taking safety, services, and resources from the rest of us. Yet the underclass is getting only the meager scraps it needs to stay alive and multiply. It is not getting what it needs to stop being underclass.

In an age of cynicism and cyclical recession, the "common humanity" argument is least persuasive as a motive force for the classes above the underclass. Yes, we may all be cut from the same cloth; still, if mine is brocade and yours is a tattered rag, I'm sorry about that, but I have a fax to send before lunch. Occasionally, forced by a circumstance or a headline, we do see that the least of us are ghostly emblems for the rest of us, the underclass haunting us with their presence. No one is without vulnerability, and the weak remind the strong of theirs. It is so easy to persecute in the underclass the tendencies we fear in ourselves: idleness, susceptibility to drugs and alcohol, surrender to immediate gratification, all the chaotic pleasures of undiscipline. These are hardly the exclusive property of any single class, but in the underclass they are so undisguised, so easily blameable. Through condemnation, we defend ourselves against our own ghosts. While the weak remain helpless, the strong remain barricaded. Yet their flesh *is* ours, and ours *is* prey to any pestilence theirs is. See AIDS.

The inescapable truth awaiting me at the end of my journey is that the underclass—underfed, undereducated, underhoused, underemployed—corrodes the foundations of our society. Even if welfare were totally eliminated, there would still be the other costs an underclass inflicts on the society at large: police, medicine, courts, hospitals, and prisons. In the absence of welfare, these costs would all increase markedly. This price, measured in the annual hundreds of billions it costs to maintain the very poor, sharply answers those who contend that the underclass is only its *own* damned problem, not ours. Being below the workforce, they cannot even obtain the old scutwork jobs traditionally associated with menial labor because most of those jobs no longer exist. In my travels among the persistently poor I kept running into men who had at one time or another been hired to dig graves. How much longer before even the last attentions of the living to the dead become automated?

The underclass forms a kind of social black hole, sucking toward it all those in the multitudes of the working poor who pass nearby. Perhaps the worst irony is that in good times the underclass falls further behind. The '80s swelled the underclass, who were shunted off and could not keep pace with changes in the way the economy functioned. The underclass sinned not only by not making it but by actually getting poorer in the supply-sided decade, the me-first decade.

Decades often pay for their predecessors. The '30s Depression was the flip side of the '20s margin-and-credit hollow boom. The wartime '40s paid for the blindness and appeasement of the '30s. The

'80s rescued the malaise of the '70s, but its prosperity was achieved at the expense of the expendables, those who were technologized, circumscribed, fenced, and finally housed out of the decade. Funds for public housing were cut by 80 percent during the '80s; the underclass grew accordingly. When we consider the underclass in the environment of an entire culture and its ideals, a giant blunder hovers over our landscape.

What to do.

Combating extreme poverty involves national leadership and specific business initiatives that promote positive action instead of resigned inertia.

Enter the government. I have come to think of the government role as limited—I will deal presently with what I mean by business initiatives—but public policy is as indispensable to countering this domestic threat as it would be with a foreign threat. Besides instructing government constitutionally to provide for the common defense, we've also given it the mission of insuring domestic tranquility, establishing justice, and promoting the general welfare. We are on record as a people. Rather than amending the Constitution, we would do better simply to read it. We would discover there the sanctity not only of property but of liberty. We have anciently enshrined both. High taxes curb both property and liberty, but so does a prosperity whose benefits are institutionally awarded only to those favored by the partnership between government and commerce.

These benefits for me mean I can write and sell this book, deduct from my income the costs of my journey through the underclass, and thereby reduce my taxes. I also take deductions for my underage children, using the savings to take them to see the Grand Canyon and my own personal favorite, the Canyon de Chelly. My wife and I have been sending them to public school for the past several years, but our Maine village, no longer possessing a high school of its own, provides part of the tuition toward private high school, which our children hope to attend. Our far-flung family, stretching from Pacific to Atlantic, plans to gather in our home next Christmas. And so on. No one who isn't poor would call us rich, but look at all the privileges our property and liberty grant us. The power to do as we please, the power of choice.

Where are the property and liberty of the underclass? They do not exist. I hope my travels and this book have made that clear.

As one of the truths he held self-evident, Thomas Jefferson wrote James Madison that "The earth is given as a common stock for man to labour and live on. If, for the encouragement of industry we allow it to be appropriated, we must take care that other employment be furnished to those excluded from the appropriation. If we do not the fundamental right to labour the earth returns to the unemployed." The underclass I have come to know is dispossessed utterly of the earth. It is not that "we" owe "them." That way lie only guilt and apathy. It is instead, if you believe Jefferson, that the underclass is being denied a kind of "fundamental right" to what the earth offers. Without nurture, education, training, and, at a minimum, decent housing, the underclass can no more "labour the earth" than a child can touch the moon.

Therefore, if we are to insure domestic tranquility in a context of justice and welfare—the very goals established by Jefferson's generation—we want to make government work to that end. The rights of children should be a crucial affair of state. If they are in persistently poor families, children become the unarmed enemy of the rights, security, and privileges the rest of us enjoy. It takes only time and neglect to turn them into the armed enemy. Most of us begin our education the first time an adult holds us, sings a song, cranks a mobile toy, or even just smiles above our cribs. The underclass needs no less. At the Parent Child Center in Chicago, which is supported by a combination of federal and local funds, I saw underclass babies actually being nurtured this way. Yet far from a demand to make such services universal, the political mood is to withdraw from these programs.

The minority constituency that elects and lobbies the executive and legislative branches has removed itself farther than ever from the underclass. In the corridors of power lip service is no longer paid to the pain of extreme poverty. While it is refreshing to see hypocrisy

vanish, what has taken its place is frightening. No official acknowl-
edgment is even grunted forth of how devastated we ourselves would
be if we could not feed, clothe, or educate our children, if we were in
danger of losing them along with our jobs, cars, and homes. When
we turn momentarily to the lives of the underclass, it is as though
these calamities were being visited upon creatures from Neptune.
Their flesh and ours might as well have different molecular structures.

The stormy debate over federal versus local administration of
poverty funds and programs is almost irrelevant in the absence of
commitment. If we understand the existence of deep poverty as a
national threat, we will act with conviction as a nation to combat it.
Until then we will continue arguing about who is responsible while
the underclass—and the crisis—grows. Just as there is no single
solution for persistent poverty because the underclass is composed of
individuals with different kinds of needs and problems, localities
also have different problems and agendas. Local solutions are necessary. The federal government, remote from localities, cannot end
poverty; what it can do is define the problems and provide leadership
toward the solutions.

"Ending welfare as we know it"—the political slogan that has
become a mantra—is the wrong goal and is doomed to fail. Instead,
the debate should be over ending poverty as we know it. This would
be a starting point for a rational policy that could have some possibility of success. Welfare programs have at times added to the
problem not because they foster indolence or encourage illegitimacy
but because they are at cross-purposes. The cash you receive, for
instance, from Aid to Families with Dependent Children, is reduced
if you also receive food stamps, leaving you no better off than before
you had the stamps. Similarly, when both unemployed parents are
present at home and neither is disabled, the children are ineligible for
AFDC; worse, if the father obtains a low-income job, his family may
lose all forms of welfare assistance. Official U.S. policy, therefore,
encourages the father to leave home. Ending welfare as we know it

becomes a sensible goal only when we decide to make welfare into a vehicle for ending poverty as we know it.

In general, Americans prefer that work be done by those who are given public assistance. Surely it is reasonable to wean people from welfare to jobs. But if it is imperative that a working society expect something in return for welfare, it may also be imperative that we need to change the definition of what kind of work to expect. Productive activity, in order for the underclass to do it, needs a less restrictive definition than many of us have been willing to grant it. Community service fans out in many directions: stacking books in libraries, separating recyclable garbage, serving refreshments at civic functions, cleaning up after such functions (where unions are not the primary contractors), attending the ill or disabled, helping other poor people with tasks or services they need but cannot perform for themselves. In this setting, 'workfare' becomes a productive activity conducive to both individual and general welfare.

But there is a point at which the welfare structure and the class structure intersect, each touching bottom, and this is where I have taken most of my soundings. We should probably call the persistently poor the permanently poor. In my bleaker moments I thought of the people I came to know not as temporarily but terminally unemployed. The third-generation jobless, pregnant teenagers, addicts, children of missing or drugged parents, alcoholics, illiterates who are over 30, mothers with disabled children, the emotionally unstable, dropouts, the marginally retarded, the aged indigent. Politicians running for office on slogans of "We work, why don't they?" literally do not know whom or what they are talking about. That is why 'workfare' remains an abstraction rather than an attainable goal.

First, most of the people I travelled among are not even educated enough to be receiving the full welfare benefits they are legally entitled to. Second, most of them are truly unable to function on a 'regular job' in the way we generally define regular job. Third, many of those who want to work have not developed the skills necessary in today's labor market. Fourth, the remainder who want to work cannot find a job that will provide day care/health care, and allow them to keep their families fed, clothed, and housed. Push these millions off welfare and the homeless population explodes, available hospital beds disappear, and prisons bulge.

To point out this reality is not to claim there are no welfare cheats. Of course there are, just as there are middle- and upper-class Americans who cheat on their taxes, thereby living in part off the rest of us. But politicians don't get elected by yelling about how vigilant they're going to be with corporate and millionaire tax evaders. So we're targeting welfare cheats.

I did actually see a Cadillac screech to a halt in front of a welfare office in Oakland. It was a dozen years old, dented everywhere, missing three hubcaps and the rear bumper, but it was still a Cadillac. The woman who climbed out of it refused to talk to me, rushed into the welfare office, and a few minutes later rushed out, again refusing even a brief chat with me. I heard stories of individuals receiving three welfare checks, claiming they had more children than were actually in their homes, still collecting for relatives a couple of years after their deaths. I don't want my taxes going to these cheats, and I assume no one else does either. Let's ferret them out. Most of these cheats are not part of the underclass. They have higher standards of living, more education, more of a work history, more enterprise, fewer disabilities than the underclass I now know. Getting rid of them, getting them off the public dole, will be wonderful, but it will not solve either the welfare problem or the underclass problem.

We are now—it is 1995 as I conclude this chronicle—literally all over the lot in our consideration of poverty. Never have our politics and our needs been so at odds. According to a nationwide network of food banks, 26 million Americans—all of them needy, not all in the impacted underclass—rely on food pantries, soup kitchens, emergency feeding programs. Many are frequently turned away because the cupboards of such places are bare. Half of these clients are children. Will we cut these programs some more and see what happens?

Like my home in Maine, this book has endured a number of climates. When I began visiting the extreme poor, George Bush was president. Although Aid to Families with Dependent Children was a program solidly in place, public housing was stalled, job training was being cut, and the general level of government attention to poverty was something like that of a child snoozing through a class that bores him. I continued my journey during the early presidency of Bill Clinton, who offered various attitudes to the poor. Compassion in the morning, decreased aid to the poor in the afternoon, increased access to education in the evening. Though they never promised programs remotely resembling, for instance, Lyndon Johnson's war on poverty, the Clintons advocated universal medical care, job re-training, and welfare reform. Little happened. The underclass problems came no closer to solution. There has been a lot of talk: what we talk about when we talk about the poor.

As I finish my journey in 1995, Bill Clinton is still president but Newt Gingrich's conservatism has set the national tone. The air is iced with talk of orphanages, work camps, cutting all aid to mothers and their children, cutting school lunches, cutting aid to legal immigrants. Cutting everywhere, building nowhere. Every utterance retro and pinched. Mothers are to blame, fathers are largely exempt. The conservative agenda is not without its appeal among the poor themselves. Along with oaths of revulsion to all politicians that are found among the middle class as well, I have heard underclass admiration for the establishment, Democratic and Republican, in almost the same terms at both ends of the country.

"He's the last liberal, Bill Clinton is," a white drifter in Bangor told me, "and he's still in there fighting for the underdog. But you have to hand it to Newt Gingrich for wanting to get the government off our backs, rich and poor. The rich man has to feel free to invest or else he won't open his wallet to hire fellas like me." A black man in line for day work in Los Angeles told me he liked Gingrich's style.

"Look, Newt's built himself a head of steam right now, and you like to see somebody filling his britches like that. He's trying to get everyone to see they're responsible for themselves, don't look for no Uncle Sam to bail you out. Yet and still, the only man back there looking out for the poor is Bill C, can't see nobody else got me in mind even 10 minutes a month."

Neither man had ever voted in an election. Both thought voter registration rolls were a way for the government to track people down and harass them. The black man's teenaged daughter, who had brought him to the job line in a car so damaged I couldn't see how it ran, said she had no respect for anyone who had ever been elected to anything. "They all be crooks and they telling us homies to straighten out while they got their hands in everybody's pocket that walks by, especially poor folks' pockets." In this young black woman's mistrust of government is the conservative agenda itself: Downsize the state.

There is some value in this current of negativity regarding poverty as well as in the rise of conservatism, however long that may last. Conservatives are finally free to try out their ideas, and liberals are free to be liberals, released from the engine of responsibility. Liberalism out of power means progressive thought is unchained. Liberals don't have to pretend they are somebody else, and radicals don't have to be nice to them. As it has become fashionable to be radical on the right, it will be permissible again to be radical on the left. As there is a taxpayers' revolt against welfare for the poor stimulated by the right, there may also come one from the left focusing on the military budget along with welfare for the rich in the form of corporate giveaways and capital gains tax breaks. Things will be looser for a while, more anarchic, but the liberals brought that on with their adherence to structures that had outlived their usefulness. The conventional liberal agenda went as far as it could with poverty anyway, ultimately exhausting itself.

Conservatism takes its turn with the underclass. In the early going, conservatives have talked more about rejecting the poor than about ending their poverty. The initial programs appear more antigovern-

ment than solution-oriented. Liberals have taken up defensive positions on the perimeter of old doctrines instead of looking ahead to
strategies that might actually eliminate the problems. The 1995
weather has Democrats in disarray, Republicans searching for cheap
fixes on social issues. In this climate, where the persistently poor I've
been traveling among are concerned, government is not only clueless
but hopeless.

If war is too important to be left to the military, persistent poverty is
too important to be left to the government. Government can only do
what it can do about poverty, it cannot demolish the underclass.
Rescuing some of the disadvantaged with emergency programs,
sponsoring early education, and legislating equal opportunity are jobs
the government can do decently if we instruct it to, but it does a terrible
job of redeeming the persistently poor. The numbers and wretched-
ness of the underclass grow as they sink farther below the rest of us.
Government will always have its crucial role in the allocation of
resources to specific programs, but it cannot solve the underclass
problem alone even if the political will is much firmer than it is halfway
through the '90s.

Enter business, the business of America.

Genuflection to the bottom line is the order of the day, from university presidents to arts committee members to the few remaining
Marxist philosophers. The business of America can be assumed to be
business at least as much as when Calvin Coolidge first made the claim
in the '20s. If we are thinking of ways to combat the threat posed by the
underclass, why don't we find out if business can help in the places and
ways where government has not?

Let's see if capitalists don't cultivate capitalism far more effectively
than civil servants do. Let's see if entrepreneurs don't promote
initiative better than bureaucrats whose own training often sup-
presses it and promotes docility. Where is it written that drug dealers
must be the most visible entrepreneurs in the slums? The complaint is
made frequently that the underclass, particularly the urban poor, lives
in a socialist third world economy where so many of the resources flow
from the welfare system that the individual becomes dependent on the

apparatus of the state. The comparison has its limitations, but let it stand. If a market economy is a good idea for Kiev, why not for the South Side of Chicago?

Corporations have expertise in many skills the underclass lack, from making and marketing to buying and selling to spreadsheets and word processing to simply showing up on time for work. The very poor do not lack the profit motive; they do lack the profit habit. For an economic system based on profit to succeed, the organizations that come together for profit—businesses—have to succeed. That is not hard for the persistently poor to learn, but they haven't had the right teachers. Aside from money, what the poorest poor lack most is contact with those who do meaningful work in what the rest of us regard as a conventional commercial environment. Corporations in ghettos could recast the relationship in America between power and the powerless so that the inaccessible could become the possible. Only business itself can go into business in the ghettos.

When proposals surface for corporations to enter ghettos, business executives have been more receptive than their critics acknowledge. They do raise, however, two principal objections to greater involvement. First, they say, we're not groupings of altruists. We manufacture garage doors or sell office supplies or design legal software. What do we know about teaching illiterates? Second, they say, we're already making more contributions to the slums than we can afford; the stockholders would be justified in changing the management team if we try to do any more.

I have heard those kinds of objections from business executives, too, but I have also found several other elements in their sensitivity to the underclass. Among corporate leaders I canvassed after completing my journey through the underclass, there is a quickened sense of poverty's urgency, a realization that urban problems have leapt into their own suburban sanctuaries, and a sense that international uncertainties will make the 21st century a bleak one for business in the absence of a fully trained American labor force. This kind of awareness is widespread. It provides fertile soil for creative plans that would bring business into the ghetto in both educational and entrepreneurial ways. As one experienced observer of corporate behavior told me, "It is in the long-term interests of corporations to help solve social problems, because otherwise capitalist societies may simply choke on their own greed."

Experimental adoption of ghetto schools is one hopeful first step a number of corporations are taking. Another is the job fair, where employers look for inner-city employees. A third is the promotion of small, almost street corner, enterprises by "downtown" executives. The presence of businesspeople in their midst effectively says to the persistently poor, All right, here's how you do what we need you to do to become someone we need.

Voluntarism has evolved into a dirty word, frequently used to excuse the abdication of public responsibility in favor of private charity. Public responsibility abides. The trouble with private charity is it generally treats symptoms instead of causes. As worthwhile as it is to provide the needy with food, clothing, and shelter, this does not attack the root cause of their need. Even if one assumes that a cause of poverty is rooted in the capitalist system itself—a defensible assumption as long as one remembers that noncapitalist societies have not been free of poverty either and have produced markedly less general prosperity than American capitalism—the individual and collective efforts of capitalists to combat poverty are essential. Business involvement in poverty should not be dismissed as the occasional act of volunteers but as the necessary fulfillment of the responsibilities of citizenship.

During wartime, business has proved it can work with government. Why not during peacetime? The point is to get American business to convey economic literacy to those who are without it and currently have no way of acquiring it. Public–private partnerships in combating poverty offer an opportunity to do this. In an Oregon program known as Jobs Plus, the state approaches businesses to find paying jobs for those on welfare. For up to six months, federal welfare and food stamp funds are used to pay the new jobholder, with the hope that at the end of this period the employer will hire the former welfare recipient full-time. The government also pays child care and medical benefits, helping with transportation costs and sometimes even with new clothes. Jobs Plus provides only entry-level, minimum-wage work, but it's a beginning and it beats sitting at home.

Wisdom and justice can scarcely be said to reside exclusively in the workings of capital. Capitalists have cheerfully participated in a century unique in its expressions of rapacity and aggression. But business does some things extremely well. In a capitalist economy, business shows you which way is up.

So much is said about role models; when businesspeople, white and black and Hispanic, become a recruiting presence in poor neighborhoods, they will be filling the need for success stories other than drug dealers, gang leaders, and—because so few can ever profitably enter these fields—athletes and entertainers. The world-class workforce a world-class economy demands can be created in part from the underclass. It cannot be created without the businesses it will be intended to serve. The Chicago teenagers I spent a night with are reclaimable; likewise the Bangor school-skippers who gathered around the statue of Paul Bunyan. They can work if only they know how. Business has the know-how. American business has always maintained it is the can-do element of society. The challenge to business leaders is to enter underclass areas and can-do their well-groomed heads off. If nothing happens to alter the course of the teenagers I was with all over the country, by the time they are 30 they will have become, like so many others I met, human driftwood.

Now: Let's get real. I did find a few business executives who were doing something about the lives of the underclass. I did not find a pattern of enlightenment spreading like a benign contagion through American business. The available evidence is that most Americans, in corporations, government, and education, are still doing business as usual. Meanwhile, the underclass multiplies.

Scavenging for a bare existence is, as with creatures of the jungle and forest, the job description of the underclass, and it is a full-time occupation. American society devotes far more resources to poverty painkillers such as food stamps and welfare, than to potential cures like early childhood intervention, educational outreach, and job training. It is estimated that for every dollar spent on Head Start, for instance, between $4 and $6 are saved on remedial schooling, criminal prosecution, and welfare. The vast majority of underclass teenage mothers have never had family-planning classes, nor do they receive prenatal care. Nor do their children go on to Head Start. Nor are the children in after-school programs such as those sponsored by Jubilee West in Oakland. Nor are the mothers in classes like Avancé's in San Antonio. Nor are the fathers anywhere in the structure of responsibility. While we turn away, persistent poverty deepens and reproduces. It will not fix itself.

The programs I have watched working are limited, which hardly means they are worthless. On the contrary, they need both support and growth. The danger is that the country is falling into a lazy, simplistic trance where the poor are concerned. We don't say, Let them eat cake; in our acute anxiety about looking out for our own selves, we say, Let them look out for themselves. Morally this may be debatable; economically, it is disastrous; and, in terms of the multiplication of human suffering, it spreads blight and rage that are infectious.

Being caught in the underclass does not mean there is no change in the lives of the very poor. The men and women I came to know were able to make significant improvements in their lives when help was available. Otherwise, they were not. The improvement was hardly a straight line on a graph. Ronnielee Divine of Oakland did "slide back," in her neighbor Irma Adkins' phrase, to using cocaine. But she also continued to receive help from a counselor at Jubilee West, and she stopped using again, and she did not lose her children. The last I heard of her, she was all dressed up in a blue suit and red shoes, going to a receptionist's job at an advertising agency in downtown Oakland. Irma Adkins was unable to raise the money to buy her house, which was sold to someone else, and she has moved out of the neighborhood she wanted to stay in. She did receive a grant to help her relocate, and she continues to work as a foster parent.

Kelso Dana, Jr. is no longer sleeping at the Bangor shelter and now has his own apartment. Although he and his girlfriend Polly aren't living together, he remains involved with her and shares parental care for their son. He is doing volunteer work at a soup kitchen, drives his own pickup truck, and participates sporadically in a job-training program. He receives Supplemental Security Income for his emotional instability, which he definitely needs, but he is described by a case-worker who has known him for years as "the most stable I've ever seen Kelso."

The Bangor shelter, after almost closing during a severe local recession, was able to expand its services to stay open around the clock. A state funding increase of less than $10,000 in 1994 made a dramatic improvement possible. No longer just a place to spend the night, the shelter offered counseling, computer and other education classes, and it provided help in finding apartments and getting medical care. Then, in 1995, a state funding cut imperiled the gains. Susan Brainerd, the shelter's director, told me the new services were in jeopardy and might have to be discontinued. Like most other shelters, there was no ongoing guarantee of funds for the Bangor shelter from any source.

Dinah Lou Freeman, the single mother of three young sons at the Parent Child Center in Chicago, went to a job fair and was hired for a trainee program at a software firm. After six months the job became permanent, but she knows she can be laid off in any business slow-down. She uses a combination of child care, a supervised after-school program, and her own sentry duty to keep her sons away from the two tables where candy and drugs are peddled in the housing project where she still lives. Hoping to leave the projects, she has not made enough money to finance a private apartment. Her hold on working-class status is precarious.

The vagabond father at Alazan Apache, Hector Zacario, is probably too old to appeal to private business or to be reached by any public reclamation project. In this way, Zacario is like much of the underclass who are past 30; no one is interested in him. He was, however, scooped up into a mandatory class for delinquent fathers run by a social agency. When I went to San Antonio in early 1995, I couldn't find him, but I heard he had recently been at his son's grade school soccer game. He was making a bet on the outcome and, characteristically, was betting against his son's team. Old Pap Finn would have bet against Huck, too. The class in fatherhood could not hold Zacario's interest, and he stopped going. In a sense, he had dropped out of the fatherhood class many years before.

A section of Alazan Apache was undergoing a hopeful renovation, with new thick walls and fresh windowpanes everywhere. This was not the section where Hector Zacario's sister is taking care of his children. In the broken-down part of Alazan Apache—boarded-up windows, graffiti on the pocked walls—the aunt was out and Hector Zacario was away. I asked a man I'd seen with Zacario where he was. "He's out of town in a two-day card game, drinking." Does he win? "He can't even win when he cheats." Isn't it dangerous to cheat in a card game? "Hector's gonna get himself cut, man. Like a car that's totaled. Any day. But if he can make it back to Alazan Apache, he'll die here."

When he does he will be no martyr, merely an unnoticed blip on the underclass radar.

It is no easier to shed preconceptions that have buttressed us than to undress in public. With our preconceptions intact, we keep the underclass not only under but outer—outside the realms of our feeling and thought. Approaching the end of his Four Quartets, T. S. Eliot anticipated the end of a journey:

If you came this way,
Taking any route, starting from anywhere,
At any time or season,
It would always be the same: you would have to put off
Sense and notion.

Eliot escorts us to a place where we are freshly shorn of predilection and tired response. For me this also means that if you put off former "sense and notion" and come to know the underclass, you will feel something you did not feel before.

Going among the underclass was the adventure of my life. It stretched me, enlarged my own circumference of perception, more than any other journey I have taken, external or internal. When I returned from a trip to San Antonio and Chicago, my then 12-year-old daughter greeted me by declaring, "You've had a near-death experience." She did not ask; she asserted. I started to reassure her but saw immediately it wasn't necessary because she was unafraid. A simple hug would do. "Near-death" is always transforming, is it not? No doubt that's what the adventure of my life means.

In a culture that values independence as much as ours, we have made it easy to shun others simply in the name of privacy. When we add the unpleasantness of poverty, the pain and guilt we cannot avoid when we watch suffering, it is not surprising we look away. Turning our backs on the underclass, we have told them to fend for themselves, that is the American way. Hardship is good for your constitution and toughens your fiber, we say, without regard for environments where a constitution is desiccated long before it can develop any but the most stunted fiber. Most of us do not think of the underclass as men and women like ourselves, with children like our own, with needs and wants fully comparable to those we satisfy daily. Nothing over the centuries has been so unremittingly urged upon the poor as the virtue of hardship by those who will not have to endure it. The irony is that deprivation, far from building character, can everywhere be seen to undermine it, to encourage cynicism and despair.

What is to be done about the underclass involves power in America concerning itself with the powerless, and some power resides in everyone who is not powerless. While the powerful vacillate, the danger from the powerless grows. The underclass can be transformed only by a national, a local, and a personal commitment.

We are talking about at least 12 to 15 million Americans, the persistently poor, with perhaps 60 million more affected directly by the vacuum in our consciousness where poverty is concerned. The underclass threat is greatest to the class just above them, the working poor, who are never out of danger from recession, automation, cheap immigrant labor, job flight to foreign countries. The rest of us watch our social services consumed by the pressing, clamorous, incessant needs of the very poor.

But can we afford to eradicate deep poverty? The answer is another question: Can we afford not to? The problem we try so hard not to look at refuses to vanish. A final question remains: Will the persistently poor and the society that rejects them slumber into the new millennium until the hour arrives at last when we are forced to reckon with each other, or will their dreams awaken us?

Concluding his final Quartet, T. S. Eliot, hardly a champion of the dispossessed himself, could nonetheless generalize his experience in a guiding way:

> We shall not cease from exploration
> And the end of all our exploring
> Will be to arrive where we started
> And know the place for the first time.

As I have come to appreciate the reality of the underclass, I have also come to appreciate my own better. As I have needed the underclass to validate my experience, I hope I have also validated theirs. Individually and collectively, they endure. With a national will that begins with national consciousness, we can do the underclass the favor, both before and beyond policy or program, of considering them human.

Acknowledgments

In order to begin knowing the people of the underclass, I needed help from many sources. With the encounters in this book occurring in the north, south, east and west, my gratitude itself fans out in all directions. Many people around the country told me where to look and among whom, sometimes even pointing me toward a specific street or housing project or social agency. The foremost among these are Renee Tajima, Michael Taylor, Mary Ann Chalila, Karen Freel, Armando Pena, Don Falk, Judy Alexander, Calvin Philips, Alfred Ramirez, and Gloria Rodriguez. Robert Greenstein of the Center on Budget and Policy Priorities, Margaret Weir of the Brookings Institution, John Elwell of the Wadleigh School Project, and the staff of the Children's Defense Fund shared with me their expertise in poverty studies. Ellie Baugher of the Census Bureau was helpful not only in providing me with useful statistics on poverty but also, more crucially, helping me understand what the numbers mean. I could not have proceeded without the early editorial scrutiny of my friends Tony Kiser, Richard Marek, Jennifer Hadley, and the late Nan Trotter, who all nudged along embryonic versions of the manuscript. The impatient patience and shrewd advice of my agent, Amanda Urban, are two of her legendary virtues, and I am happy to affirm the legend. Maria denBoer's copyediting is, like my software, word perfect. Finally, Emily Loose is a dream editor, mixing clarity of thought with perceptive criticism with limitless encouragement. I am grateful to all for their help, hopeful only that they will not feel their guidance and counsel were misplaced.